Y0-DJM-594

THEY HELPED ME ESCAPE:
From Amsterdam to Gibraltar in 1944

THEY HELPED ME ESCAPE:
From Amsterdam to Gibraltar in 1944

by Clayton C. David

Sunflower University Press®
1531 Yuma (Box 1009), Manhattan, Kansas 66502-4228

Copyright 1988 by Clayton C. David

ISBN 0-89745-101-5

Layout
Lori L. Daniel

Introduction

With his battle-damaged B-17 on fire as a result of a two and a half hour air battle, which had seen his group fight its way to the target and back on 11 January 1944, copilot Clayton C. David parachuted to safety and landed on a dike of the Zuider Zee in enemy-controlled territory near Amsterdam, Holland. From there his life became a fascinating endeavor to evade capture in Holland, Belgium, and France to escape into Spain where he would be arrested and interned until placed in British and American hands.

The escape, which required some four and a half months, found David eye to eye with the police, receiving help from ordinary citizens, on his own at times, or being escorted by outstanding resistance workers. Although many of his known helpers paid with their lives for their part in the resistance, some survived the prisons and concentration camps. Still others went unnoticed and were never arrested.

The author and his helpers, both male and female, all had one common objective. They were in pursuit of freedom for themselves and their countries. When these survivors from both sides of the Atlantic get together, they are keenly aware of the price that was often paid to achieve freedom, but it had to be done. This story looks in on the lives of the helpers 40 years later to learn the effect that the war had on these brave people and their assisting Allied airmen.

Introduction

Acknowledgment

I see the events in our lives as primarily the result of the choices we make for ourselves or of those made for us. Some of these choices are clear and distinctly based on factual information. Some are a matter of selecting the least undesirable projected outcome, and still others are a gamble on instincts which may be influenced by a power greater than man. Happenings that are casually referred to as luck may occur as a result of being prepared to provide a power greater than man the opportunity to guide our decisions.

My decision to write this book was based on facts, observations, and the urging of others. The support and help of my loving wife, Lenora "Scotty" David, has made it possible. I wish also to acknowledge the encouragement of friends and my evasion helpers who provided much information. Thanks to Simone Scales, who was born and reared in Belgium, now living in the United States. She was most gracious in using her language skills to translate Dutch and French information for me.

Thanks also to Linda Boots Gucciardo who read the original manuscript and made valuable suggestions about its organization and style. To friends at West Virginia Northern Community College who assisted me in the use of equipment, I am grateful.

I believe that freedom is taken for granted by too many Americans and in that context it has a tendency to lose its value. The desire to have my readers understand the value of freedom when it is lost or threatened is a feeling that propelled me. The clincher was the experiences we had in 1983 and 1985 when we tried saying thanks to those who had helped me and fliers like me that were shot down and landed behind enemy lines. Every time we tried to say thanks and show appreciation to those people of the Netherlands, Belgium, and France, we found them thanking us for helping make their freedom from German control a reality.

The comradeship which exists when downed Allied airmen and their wartime helpers get together as individuals, or at a meeting of an Air Force Escape and Evasion Society, is electrifying. There is an indescribable closeness among these people who have shared the risks of death and have survived — even after years of separation.

Clayton C. David
Hannibal, MO
August 1987

Contents

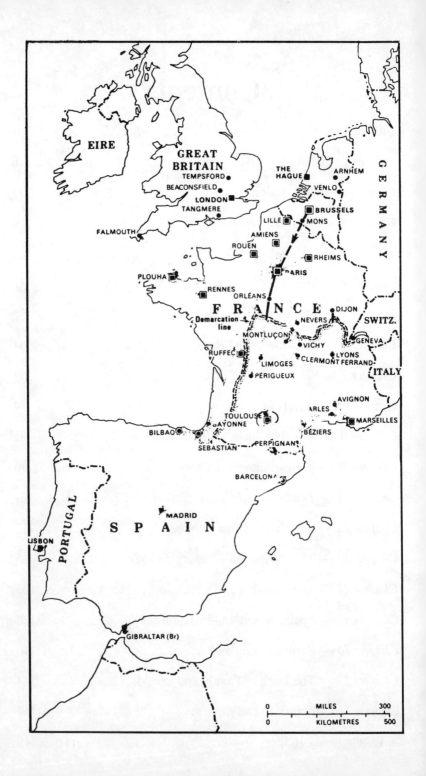

Chapter 1

Pilot Training

Learning to fly was a choice I made my senior year in college at Kansas State University in Manhattan, Kansas. The government offered classes and free flying lessons through the Civilian Pilot Training Program. The ground-school classes involved Theory of Flight, Navigation, Meterology, and Flight Regulations. The flying lessons involved eight hours in the air with an instructor, then the thrill of that first solo flight to be followed by more hours of instruction and solo flying. There were specific flying exercises and cross country flights. When the CAA Inspector wrote, "Private Pilot test passed satisfactorily," my log book showed a total of 42 hours of flight time.

My older brother, Floyd, had personally bought his flying time and earned his pilot's license. I felt fortunate that I could earn my private license with the government paying for my flying time. My license number, 78792-41, is dated 5 June 1941. Two of my close friends also participated in the program. One of them, Dale Hupe, became a Marine pilot; the other, Clifford Jackson, became a Navy pilot. If what we did with our future was any indication, the program paid off for the government.

When I learned to fly, flying combat missions was not what I was thinking about. But in the fall of 1941, as my draft number got close, flying had more appeal than the Infantry which had been the basis of my ROTC classes in college. When I took examinations for the Army Air Corps and for the Navy, I was turned down for pilot training. My eyes had been over-worked with college and long hours on a new job. The familiar letter, "Greetings from the President of the United States. You have been selected . . ." took me to the Ft. Leavenworth, Kansas, Induction Station on 1 December 1941.

That first week of December 1941 I was among a group of men who wondered why we were in service and for how long. Unity of purpose and a common goal did not seem to exist. Then came Pearl Harbor! In a few hours the Japanese had united our country for war to a degree not previously achieved in spite of President Roosevelt's efforts at preparation. On 8 December it was a new Army with a common purpose: "Let us fight it, win it, and go home!"

The next few months found me training for and performing different duties in the Medical Corps. I chose activities that would not tax my eyes in preference to detailed work that would strain them. Then I had another chance to take the mental and physical tests for the Army Air Corps, and this time I was successful and passed. This led to a transfer to Shepherd Field at Wichita Falls, Texas, to await assignment to a class of Flying Cadets. While waiting, we drilled and exercised daily in the hot Texas sun. It was summer 1942 and most of us in the company had been in the service from six months to six years — a boring experience. No other group on the base spent as much time on the obstacle course as we did.

In October 1942, I was assigned to the class of 43F in the Gulf Coast Training Command and began preflight training at San Antonio, Texas. For eight weeks we went through rigid cadet training. During the four weeks as underclassmen and four weeks as upperclassmen, we experienced mental and physical conditioning. We received first-hand exposure to discipline and learned to cope with it. My previous ground-school classes, taken to earn my private pilot's license, were very beneficial in doing my classroom work. I also found my previous experience in a college fraternity valuable. It helped me to accept the pain in my aching back when I lay down on my bunk at lights out.

From the very beginning we were told that only about one-half of the group would be successful in being accepted and passing all steps necessary to winning our wings as pilots and becoming officers. It was not surprising that some of the men quit voluntarily or were transferred out before completing preflight training. In my case, the experience increased my determination to succeed and made me more physically tough and mentally alert.

Upon completion of preflight training we were sent to various airfields to begin flight training. I was assigned to the Primary Flight School at Pine Bluff, Arkansas. There I had my first flight in a Fairchild-built PT-19A on 2 December 1942. My first flight instructor at Pine Bluff was the one who gave the periodic check rides. He informed the six of us who had been assigned to him that because we all had private pilot licenses, he knew we could fly. His duty was to see if we could fly the Army way. Before he finished with us and assigned us to other instructors (so that he could proceed with giving check rides), he washed out one of the cadets that had over 200 hours of flight time. Flying the Army way took on special meaning for me.

All phases of flight training involved ground-school classes, physical exercise, and military drill. We learned about the airplanes we flew and how to recognize enemy aircraft and ships, as well as our own and those of our Allies. Safety awareness was before us at all times, and yet accidents did occur. The temptation to enjoy the sky too much when those earthly bonds are broken can tempt a flier to take unnecessary risks. Self discipline is essential if one is to explore and stretch his skills within the limits of his knowledge and the capabilities of the airplane. But the willingness to take some calculated risks is a key in the development of leadership.

Parachutes were issued with instructions on how to use them in case you got into a situation where the condition or the position of your aircraft was such that your ability to make a safe landing seemed impossible. However, a simulated jump made from a tower was the extent of our parachute training.

Upon completion of primary flight training, we moved on to basic at Winfield, Kansas. We were exposed to the torque of a propeller on a larger engine capable of pulling you off a straight line on takeoff if you didn't correct for it. You now had a canopy covering you in the air to keep off some of the cold. There was a radio, and we got our first introduction to instrument flying and flying at night. In addition, we were spending hours in the Link trainer, which simulated instrument flying. From that time on, flying on instruments in the air and using the Link trainer would be a regular part of our training.

When we completed basic flight training we were assigned to either a twin-engine or a single-engine school for advance training. Those assigned to single-engine advance flew AT-6 aircraft and upon graduation most were sent to fighters. I went to Altus, Oklahoma, and on 30 April 1943 I had my first flight in a twin-engine aircraft, the AT-17 built by Cessna. This was preparation for flying larger airplanes, which meant bombers for most of us.

On 26 June 1943, I proudly put on my silver wings as a pilot and accepted my commission as a Second Lieutenant in the Army of the United States. After graduation I had a few days at home near Topeka,

Kansas, and then it was off to Pyote, Texas, to begin combat-crew training as a copilot on the B-17 Flying Fortress. That four-engine plane was considered a large aircraft at the time. At Pyote it was easy to concentrate on flying and crew training because there was not much chance for distractions with the schedule we had and no towns nearby.

This was the beginning of our training in the type of aircraft we could expect to carry us into combat. For the first time we came together as a crew and were expected to develop into a team. Prior to this, each of the ten men had been trained for specific duties. Now, that training had to blend together on a single aircraft so that the skills of each man could contribute to the over-all objectives of the missions we would be assigned. Each man had to be able to skillfully perform his primary assignment and help another when necessary. All men needed general knowledge about the aircraft.

A crew usually consisted of four commissioned officers and six non-commissioned officers. Our crew was composed in that manner. After graduation from cadets, our pilot, like most, had received special training in the B-17 and was checked out as pilot. My first exposure to the B-17 was my assignment as copilot. We two pilots had to understand the operation of the airplane and work together to fly it.

The other two officers on the crew were the navigator and the bombardier. Each had graduated from cadets with special training including air time and gunnery training. They shared the compartment in the nose of the airplane. In simple terms, the navigator was expected to guide the pilots to the target area so that the bombardier could deliver the bombs on the target. They assisted each other when needed and saw that one or the other could man the guns in the nose of the plane at all times. Their compartment was forward and below that of the pilots.

Close by to the rear of the pilots was the flight engineer, who had mechanical training and gunnery experience. He was expected to keep an eye on certain instruments and relay information to or interpret it for the pilots. He also checked mechanical aspects of the airplane before takeoff and exchanged information with the ground crew that maintained the airplane. In combat, he operated the top gun turret.

Going from the nose back, the next compartment was the bomb bay which physically separated the five men in the front of the plane from the five at the rear. A narrow catwalk through the center, where bombs were hung on either side, provided access to the next compartment, which was the radio room. The technically trained radio operator had an overhead gun, which he manned in addition to his radio equipment.

The compartment behind the radio room was the most open part of the airplane. From there you could enter the ball turret, which hung below the plane. It was only occupied by the ball-turret gunner during flight. The tail of the airplane was equipped with twin guns operated by the tailgunner. He, too, took his position only in flight. The main door used to enter or exit the rear of the airplane was located on the side of this large compartment called the waist.

Both the right and left sides of the waist had a .50-caliber machine-gun mounted in it. A man was assigned to each gun, and they were referred to as "waist gunners." On our crew, one of these men also had training as a radio operator. The other one had mechanical training as an engineer. Although all of the non-commissioned officers were trained in aerial gunnery and could have alternated to another gun if necessary, the ball-turret gunner and the tailgunner were located in critical positions difficult to get to and it would be a rare situation for either to leave his guns for another position during combat.

Each man had the responsibility for maintaining his guns and having a supply of ammunition. Each person also needed to understand the critical aspects of the area of the airplane where he was stationed and how he and the aircraft might be affected by possible battle damage.

Our training from this time forward would be designed to increase the proficiency of each man and the crew as a team. Classroom courses and physical training continued along with our time in the air. Our flight-training missions involved many takeoffs and landings, including emergency procedures. There were navigational flights day and night along with practice bombing missions and gunnery practice. We spent hours in flying formation with other bombers to improve our skills and to give the crew a feel for that type of flying. Flying high altitude on oxygen was an important exercise. We also practiced emergency bail out procedures in the air and on the ground. In the air we did not leave the airplane, but on the ground we did and often timed how long it took us to execute an emergency exit. There were over water training flights in the Gulf out of the sight of land to prove our navigator's ability and to expose the crew to future situations.

Before completing our combat training and leaving the United States, we went through three phases of training. Phase one at Pyote was followed with two additional phases at Dyersburg, Tennessee. After that we were sent to staging for preparation to being shipped overseas. I was lucky that our staging took place at the air base at Topeka, Kansas, which was only a few miles from my home. It gave me one last chance to spend some time with my parents before leaving the United States.

From the time we started our combat-crew training at Pyote the objective was always clear. We were told: "You can expect to be flying daylight bombing missions from England. Your ability to fly a tight formation and function as a team is critical." It was generally understood that, if as a team you were good at your job, and lucky, you had about one chance in four or five of completing 25 combat missions and returning to the United States in a year or less. Even if you were good, you could have the misfortune of being shot down by flak or fighters. If shot down there was still hope, if you landed safely: "Some people have been fortunate enough to land in an occupied country and escape."

The primary goal then was to be the best you can be and complete 25 missions. The secondary goal: To know and do the right things to try to escape if you must bail out or crash-land in enemy occupied territory. The successful achievement of either goal required sufficient training and knowledge to believe in yourself, your crew, the power of divine guidance and a lot of luck. Training and knowledge properly applied are great confidence builders to guide behavior in a crisis or an emergency.

We boarded the *Queen Elizabeth* at New York on 2 November 1943 to cross the Atlantic unescorted. The ship's Captain and his superiors were betting on the speed of that fantastic British liner to avoid the German U-boats. The only drawback about my stateroom was sharing it with 20 other officers. That was a fact of life when a cruise ship was converted to a troop ship. On 9 November we were in the quiet harbor at Glasgow, Scotland. It was such a tranquil site that except for the thousands of us going ashore, it certainly lacked the environment of a war.

On 17 November 1943, our training crew was assigned to the 358th

Squadron of the 303rd Bomb Group at Molesworth, England. We had become a part of the First Division of the Eighth Air Force. The crew was listed as follows:

Position	Rank/Name	Number
P	2nd Lt. Karl B. Arundale	0742551
CP	2nd Lt. Clayton C. David	0682818
B	2nd Lt. James F. Barlow	0752544
N	2nd Lt. Joe B. Vogel	0676182
AEG	Sgt. Angelo P. Petix	13107303
ROG	S/Sgt. Richard A. Davis, Jr.	18118979
AAEG	Sgt. Charles C. Finch	34393652
AROG	Sgt. James T. Elovich	31192480
AG	Sgt. Joseph F. Fertitta	18190215
AAG	Sgt. Theodore R. Czeczotka	12188200

At Molesworth it did not take long to realize that this was the place where continued training and combat came together in the realities of war.

For their first combat mission, newly assigned pilots and copilots often found themselves in the copilot seat next to a pilot who had already survived some combat flying. Thus I found myself flying as copilot with a crew that had been on some previous missions. The assignment came suddenly when the copilot of that crew was unable to answer his mission wake-up call because of a back injury sustained in a minor truck accident the night before.

I still considered myself a member of the crew with which I had trained in the States, and I did brief with them for a mission to Berlin that was scrubbed before takeoff. However, my combat missions were flown with pilot Lt. Jack Watson and his crew. My first mission was to Bremen, Germany, on 20 December 1943. The second was to Kiel, Germany, on 4 January 1944. Lt. Watson gave me a chance to demonstrate my ability, and between missions I was receiving additional training to be checked out as first pilot. Then came 11 January 1944. This was my third mission and the day that started the chain of events which this book is about.

Left, Cadet Clayton David is dressed to go flying in the open cockpit of a PT-19.

Below, the B-17 crew that trained together. Standing left to right are Lieutenants Arundale, David, Barlow, and Vogel. Kneeling left to right are Sergeants Finch, Elovich, Petix, Davis, Fertitta, and Czeczotka.

Chapter 2

Survival

Well before daylight on 11 January 1944, bomber crews all over England were being briefed for a maximum effort that was expected to send out the greatest number of bombers ever at this point in the war. Missions are usually planned with the expectation that most squadrons and groups will have a normal percentage of planes remaining on the ground for repairs or to fill in if some planes abort at takeoff. When an M.E. (or maximum effort) is called for, every base is expected to send out all flyable planes.

Three primary targets had been selected. More than 700 bombers were expected to participate in the day's mission. In addition to the exceptionally large number of bombers, fighters were scheduled to provide cover and protection. When the fighters flew cover, they usually flew a few thousand feet above the bomber formations looking for enemy fighters. They could then either shoot down the enemy fighters or chase them away from our bomber formations. These little friends above were a welcome sight to the bomber crews. The bomber formations contained an awesome amount of firepower, but against enemy fighters it was of a defensive nature, not the offensive weapon that our fighter escort was.

The targets that had been selected were Oschersleben, Brunswick, and Halberstadt. The only thing that was uncertain was the weather for later in the day. This was the day for the 358th Squadron to lead our 303rd Bomb Group, which was putting up 60 planes. The 303rd was leading the First Division of the Eighth Air Force. Flying in the lead plane of the 303rd, the old *Eight Ball*, was Brig. Gen. Robert F. Travis and Lt. Col. William R. Calhoun of the 41st Combat Wing. The mission would be flown as if Berlin was the target. Then about 100 miles from Berlin the formation would turn to the real target, Oschersleben, and make its bomb run.

Takeoff and assembly went as planned. As we entered the air space over the continent, the flak began to appear as expected and the

German fighters came up to press their attack. The fight was on! Then came a recall on the mission. Weather was moving in quickly on England. Our fighters would be unable to get off in large numbers as expected, to provide the intended support. In addition, our bombers returning to England later in the day would experience very hazardous landing conditions.

Not wanting to appear as if they were being turned back by the German fighters, the lead bomb groups, which were already under attack, continued on to their targets. The statistics taken from the *Mighty Eighth War Diary* by Roger A. Freeman, shows that the First Bomb Division, of which the 303rd was a part, reported as follows:

> 291 B-17 bombers were dispatched, 42 bombers did not return. Three that did return were damaged beyond economical repair and an additional 125 B-17 bombers were damaged. Ten men in the returning bombers had been killed and 29 were wounded. 430 men of the division were missing in action.

Of the 60 bombers dispatched that day from the 303rd Bomb Group, 10 did not return and 109 men were missing in action.

Life magazine, dated 24 January 1944, page 28, gave a very reliable report on the day's activities including artist conceptions of the battle. It reported:

> One of the great air battles of history took place last week. In full daylight some 700 heavy bombers of the U.S. Eighth Air Force fought their way 300 miles into northwest Germany. Their main targets were the three fighter-plane factories near Brunswick but the apparent direction of the attack toward Berlin, 100 miles away, brought hundreds of Nazi interceptors up for a three-hour running battle from the Zuider Zee to the edge of Berlin's defenses and back again.
>
> Screened by clouds for the middle part of the trip, the Fortresses and Liberators met their heaviest opposition as they approached the target area. Fanning out, the formations went after the airplane plant at Oschersleben which assembles half the FW-190s made in Germany, after the

Messerschmitt 110 factory at Brunswick and after a factory at Halberstadt that builds wings for Ju-88s. Some groups, hunting targets of opportunity, struck at the crowded freight yards at Bielefeld while scattered others may have ranged to Berlin itself. The tonnages of bombs dropped were not immediately announced.

The desperate Luftwaffe opened its full bag of defensive tricks, some new, some improved. German fighters met the U.S. planes with smokescreens, rocket barrages and "saturation" attacks. Large formations of Me-110s carrying twice their regular rocket load, fired salvos into the leading bomber flights. When rocket fire split open the tight U.S. defensive formations, Me-110s, and FW-190s followed up with ferocious close attacks.

Our planes used a new trick, too, a shuttling fighter cover that gave maximum protection. Lightnings and Thunderbolts took the bombers most of the way to the target. There the heavies met a fresh group of fighters, long-range Mustangs, that guarded them halfway home. On the last leg of the trip back, RAF Spitfires gave cover. It was the longest escort job yet for the newly improved Mustangs.

In spite of our protecting fighters, the German interceptors pressed their attacks relentlessly, often coming within 75 feet of the bombers before turning away. The heavies closed the gaps in their formations and kept on for England. Sixty U.S. bombers and five U.S. fighters were lost. The 1200-odd planes that did get back reported 152 German fighters destroyed. The number of Germans shot down by the planes that didn't return will never be known.

From the *Mighty Eighth War Diary* we learn that the First, Second, and Third Bomb Divisions dispatched a total of 663 bombers. Sixty did not return, four were damaged beyond economical repair, and 179 others were damaged. Ten men in returning bombers were dead, 34 were wounded, and 606 were missing in action. Totals on our fighter-planes were 592 dispatched, five did not return, three planes were not repaired, and six were damaged. Two men were killed and three were missing in action. (Our First Division, although supplying less than one-half the bombers, 291 of 663, suffered more than two-thirds of the losses with 440 men killed or MIA of the 616 total that were killed or missing.)

Losses took place on both sides and the damage inflicted on the Germans was an important statistic. The *Mighty Eighth War Diary* reveals our reported claims for 11 January 1944 were as follows:

Reports from —	*bomber crews*	*fighter pilots*
Enemy aircraft		
destroyed	228	31
Probably destroyed	60	12
Damaged	98	16

Although claims from the returning bomber crews were not as accurate as those of the camera carrying fighters, and may have involved some duplication, there was no accurate way to determine the number of enemy aircraft destroyed or damaged by the bomber crews that did not return.

Early in the fight our number three engine was shot out. Sitting in the cockpit, the engines were numbered from left to right. The number two engine is closest to the pilot on his left and the number three engine is on his right and nearest the copilot's position. Both engine number two and three are referred to as the inboard engines. Continued operation of engines one and four, referred to as the outboard engines, usually provides better control of the plane, and the flight characteristics are better. However, the loss of any engine obviously restricts operational capabilities. Therefore, we found it necessary to cut some corners on the triangle flown near the target so that we could drop our bombs and stay close to the formation.

Shortly after leaving the target area, our number two engine was hit. With both engines number two and three feathered to reduce drag, we were attracting German fighters. We needed all the overhead protection we could get, so we started sacrificing altitude to maintain airspeed and stay under our formation, which was flying at 23,000 feet. Bombers going down in flames and German fighters being shot out of the sky became a common sight. A few friendly fighters did arrive to give support, but the number was small. They had been affected by the weather and their dog fights.

As we entered the airspace over the Netherlands on our return, we could see low clouds moving in and obscuring our view of the ground. At this point we had given up about 8,000 feet of altitude for enough speed to keep up with the formation above us. However, with 15,000 feet of altitude and two good engines, we believed we would safely survive the battle which had now lasted for at least two and one-half hours. The navigator kept up with our position and had just reported that we were east of Amsterdam, probably over the Zuider Zee, when we suffered another attack, and fire started in the area of our number two gas tank. Pilot Watson issued the bail-out order and rang the bell to abandon our burning plane. It appeared to be the only logical thing to do before the gas tank blew up and took us spinning, as we had seen so many others do that day.

When I went below to bail out from my assigned exit for such an emergency, I was surprised to find that the bombardier had not already jumped. The pilot would be the last to leave from that exit. When I inquired of the bombardier, "Are you OK, or have you been shot?" he assured me that he was all right and said, "I'll jump after you." This he did. The navigator and flight engineer had preceded me out that exit as we had practiced on the ground many times. Other members used the side exit to the rear of the plane.

You can practice an emergency exit from a plane on the ground, but you don't practice a real jump without actually leaving the aircraft. This was our first — the ultimate test to see if we could mentally and physically execute what we had learned from lectures and briefings.

My number one goal of flying 25 missions, so that I could return to the States, had just been shattered. It was time to try for goal number two: to make a safe jump, avoid capture, and escape. At this point I was glad I had attended briefings on escape and a recent lecture by a British paratrooper. Certain instructions were now clear: "Don't worry about a falling sensation." "Delay the opening of your parachute as long as possible to decrease the chance of being seen and to increase the opportunity for evading capture."

Before leaving my seat to jump, I noted our altitude was 15,000 feet and I estimated the strata of clouds below to be about 3,000 feet. As I went out of the escape hatch, I used the same method I was accustomed to using on the ground. I sat down on the edge of the escape hatch with my feet outside and made a feet-first exit. But, instead of my feet being on the ground, the airstream of the plane was tumbling me like a ball. The paratrooper had told us to expect that, and said it could be stopped by fully extending one's arms and legs and becoming somewhat rigid. When I did this, my tumbling stopped and I found myself in control. There was no falling sensation. Except for seeing the plane above going away, and the clouds below coming up to meet me, this passing through the air at about 120 mph gave the feeling of being blown upward. There was only the noise of the wind. The roar of the plane's engines and the rattle of guns were gone.

True to myself, I waited until entering the clouds before pulling my ripcord. The parachute opened with a jerk! I looked down to see that my shoes were still on and at almost the same instant came out below the cloud cover. The silence was intense; all was calm. At first glance, I could only see water. Then I spotted a dike, and when I realized that my descent would take me into the water, I remembered another suggestion from the paratrooper: "If you want to steer your parachute, pull the shroud lines down in the direction you want to go." I did this until I was afraid that the chute might collapse, and thus for a moment I relaxed my hold. But realizing that the pull on the shroud lines was essential, I renewed my grasp and was able to hit the side of the dike on firm ground. My first phase of survival had been totally successful.

If I were to evade capture I had to destroy the evidence of my landing and find a place to hide. The water seemed to be the best place to dispose of the parachute, so I quickly removed my life vest, then my parachute harness, and rolled them all together. When I threw the bundle into the water, it floated some and began sinking much too slowly to suit me. I took off the warm flying boots I had on over my shoes, filled them with water, and tossed them on top of the parachute. Everything sank out of sight. I took time to look around and as I did, I saw other members of my crew in their billowy white chutes slowly floating out of the overcast that was within 500 feet of the ground. As they descended into the water on either side of the dike, I realized I had extended my free fall closer to the ground than I had intended, but it was for the best.

I heard the motors of boats being started to pick my crew members out of the water so that they could be taken prisoners. The delayed opening of my parachute had put me on the ground well ahead of my crew, and I had hoped that it also meant I had landed without being seen by the Germans.

As I started looking for a hiding place, I could see a farmhouse in the distance across a body of water, with people outside watching. I only had two directions I could go, and both were along the dike. At that moment a man riding a bicycle came up along the side of the dike and pointed the direction for me to run. And run I did. In a few hundred yards I came upon a field of grass. It was closely grazed and offered no protection, but the shallow drainage ditches would, so I ran out into the field to one of the ditches and lay down in two or three inches of water. My olive-drab flight suit blended with the grass on either side of the ditch, and I was not easily seen.

January in Holland is not a good time to be lying in water. The air temperature was just above freezing, and the water was about the same. It would be impossible to tolerate having most of one's body submerged in such cold water for very long, but I found I could withstand it by assuming a prone position that kept most of my body dry.

It was then about 2:00 pm and darkness would come early. I decided to lie still and wait for darkness in spite of having seen people at the farmhouse watching me as I hid. If they were not friendly, there was no way I would avoid capture in such open territory. I had to hope for the best while I lay and waited. A thousand thoughts must have gone through my mind, but the recurring questions were: What would happen to my crew members? Could I ever escape? What would my folks think when they got the telegram — Missing in Action? Would the people who saw me hide help me or report me? And, where and when will I try to go from here? Would I catch my death of cold lying here wet and cold in January?

To each question I tried to offer a rational answer and maintain my composure. As I lay there I mentally reviewed the contents of my escape kit, which was a plastic box about three inches by four inches and one-inch thick. I carried it zipped in the leg pocket of my flying suit. It contained some folding money from Germany and Holland, two silk maps made in great detail, a small compass, some chocolate, adhesive tape, matches, benzedrine and halazone tablets, and a water bag. All of these items could be helpful to me, but I would need much more, and I was very aware of that.

About 4:30 pm, before I thought it was dark enough to travel, I saw a man wearing wooden shoes starting to search in my area. It was evident he knew I was there somewhere. When he was about 30 yards away, he began a soft friendly whistle, so I raised my head enough to catch his eye and returned immediately to my fully prone position. The man came near and asked one question, "American?" I replied, "Yes," and he motioned for me to remain still. Then, this man, about five-feet, nine-inches tall and dressed in working clothes, returned to a point near the farmhouse. He came back to me promptly and indicated that I should follow him as he started toward the farmstead. It felt good to stretch my cold, wet body. We had only gone a few hundred yards when there were dogs barking and some commotion in the farmyard. I responded to my guide's hand signal to hit the deck, and found myself lying on grass covered with about one inch of water, which we had been walking in. I realized the value of wooden shoes for keeping the feet dry.

In a few minutes my guide got an all clear signal and had me up following him at a distance of ten to 15 yards. We proceeded to the barnyard and into the barn where the cows were housed adjacent to the house. From the milkbarn he opened the door into the kitchen, and I followed closely behind. There were no lights on, and only a small amount of daylight remained, which meant we would soon be under the cover of darkness. It was years later that I learned this was the Schouten farm.

Once I was inside the kitchen, my guide went to another part of the house apparently to maintain a look-out, and left me in the care of an older man who was seated at the kitchen table. I believe the women of the house were assisting with the chores and the milking, so there were just the two of us there together. I don't know his identity, or his true place in this whole picture, but this older man spoke excellent English. He had me remove my shoes, socks, outer flight suit, and the heavy electrically heated suit I had on. The suits and socks were placed in the oven to dry. I was provided with warm milk and some excellent cheese between slices of a very coarse and dry bread. I'm confident they gave me the best they could provide, but it was immediately evident by the bread that the German confiscation of food in Holland had already reached into the countryside.

While I sat there eating and waiting for my clothes to dry, the gentleman proceeded to confirm in his own mind that I was an American. Then came the sales pitch on why I should surrender to the Germans. "The Red Cross is getting food to the prison camps. It would reduce the danger to people like ourselves who run great risk in trying to help you. The war can't last too much longer. The chances of escaping are very slim." — and so it went. After more than an hour I began to lose my patience, at which time I stood up and said, "I will not surrender! If you can't help me, please don't stand in my way; I'll proceed on my own." I began recovering my socks and outer flying suit from the oven. The heavy electrically heated flying suit was still very wet, so I left it. In response, the gentleman said, "We will help you." This obviously had been a testing session. They did not want to risk their lives for a person who did not strongly believe in his ability to evade capture.

I was directed out of the kitchen to two young men who had apparently been waiting in the milkbarn to help me if I passed the test. They walked me to a location some 500 yards from the house and rowed me in a boat across a small canal to an enclosed shed about 25 feet square, sitting in the pasture field.

The shed was filled with hay and cattle. It was not easily accessible from the road because of the canal, but it was a location I could have reached by myself without assistance from the local people. As the young men bade me farewell and said they would be back before daylight, I was confident that if the Germans should find me, I could deny having had any help and be convincing about it.

Left to myself for the night, I was glad for my farm background and an understanding of cattle. Being with cattle calls for calmness to avoid a disturbance. It was cold outside, and my shoes were still wet and cold to my feet. The body heat of the cattle helped to warm the small shed, and as I lay down in the manger near them I pulled some loose hay over me. Then being reasonably comfortable, except for my feet, I decided to remove my shoes and put my feet against the side of a heifer lying near the manger. Her body was better than an old fashioned bed warmer, providing enough comfort for me to get some sleep. And the heifer didn't seem to mind.

Early the next morning, well before daylight, the two young men returned as promised and took me back across the small canal, then through the fields to a country road which we followed into a small village. I believe it was their mother who gave me breakfast. It was a good way to start the day. The weather, which had created problems for us the day before, was now giving me an advantage. It was still dark and very foggy when we left the house and walked a short distance to a rowboat that was used to take me to a small island. There

I was placed in a vacant but small house-like building and told they would return for me after dark that night.

There was some comfort in being in such an isolated place. Even so, I stayed low and kept away from the windows. I had placed my life in the hands of strangers who I knew were risking their lives to help me. The least I could do was to cooperate to the fullest.

As midday approached the fog had lifted, but the overcast remained. Finally the quiet was interrupted with the squeak of oars in their locks. I peeked out a window to see what was happening and saw a man get out of his boat and pull it on to the shore far enough to keep it safe. He then retrieved something from the boat and headed for my location. It was evident that he knew I was there. He approached a side window and I moved toward it. Then I raised it in response to his motions. He handed me a small warm bowl and reached inside his jacket to bring out a bottle of milk and an apple. He then retreated from the building and proceeded to cut some weeds while I ate a delicious meal. The warm bowl contained a small piece of roast beef with cooked carrots and potatoes.

When I finished eating I returned to the open window and the man came over to retrieve the bowl and bottle. I thanked him several times and watched him return to his boat and row away. I believe it was the only time I ever saw that gentleman, who had just risked his life to bring me a meal that I'm confident contained his week's ration of meat.

As I reclined on the floor waiting for darkness and the return of my young friends, I realized that I had survived the air battle, my parachute jump, and the first 24 crucial hours. My future was now in the hands of strangers who were befriending me at great personal risk to themselves, their families, and friends. Greater love hath no man than these people had already shown and there was much more to come.

I have never been able to learn the names of all the people who helped me during those first 30 hours, and I probably never will. However, a map supplied to me by Ida Kuipers-Bakker apparently traces my moves during those early hours in Holland. It had all occurred near the village of Durgerdam.

Piet Schouten was a farmer and the first person putting himself and his family at risk to help me. We were all fortunate that I was hidden in the cow shed in the field, because the Germans searched the house that night, but not the shed. They returned the next day and again searched the farmstead.

When we returned to the area in 1983, the house had burned and had been rebuilt. Piet Schouten and his family no longer lived there. It was as if my presence there in 1944 had been blotted out so that no one would know. On the surface it was a well-kept secret.

In 1985 we again returned to Durgerdam. Good fortune led us to the home of Jurr Bakker. This talented man, young at 78, was spending his days before a window that looks out on the street and across to the ships sailing on the Zuider Zee. While he painted and carved with unusual skill, his thoughts often took him back to World War II and his submarine duty in the Dutch Navy.

Mr. Bakker was not in Durgerdam when I passed that way in 1944, but his keen mind and a natural instinct for details had permitted him to learn about those days. When we told him I had bailed out and landed nearby, he was immediately able to tell us where I had been hidden and it confirmed what I had remembered. His comment then summed up the people and their attitude when he said, "You didn't think anyone knew you were hidden there on the island, but they all knew" — a secret well kept to protect the active participants of a real-life threatening drama. Similar acts of silence were certain to have occurred several times while I passed through The Netherlands, Belgium, and France, helping me and others evade capture.

Before we parted from Mr. Bakker and his visiting daughter, Ida C. Kuipers-Bakker, a number of people had been told by phone that their American had returned. It was as if the whole community still takes pride in the action of those individuals who had helped me, and I was a living symbol of their efforts in the darkest of days. To remember my return visit, I have my own wooden shoes carved personally by Mr. Bakker. We also have a painting of the island where I was hidden and a cloth tote bag that was decorated with one of his paintings. Our entire experience at Durgerdam in 1985 served to emphasize the character of Christian people possessed with brotherly love.

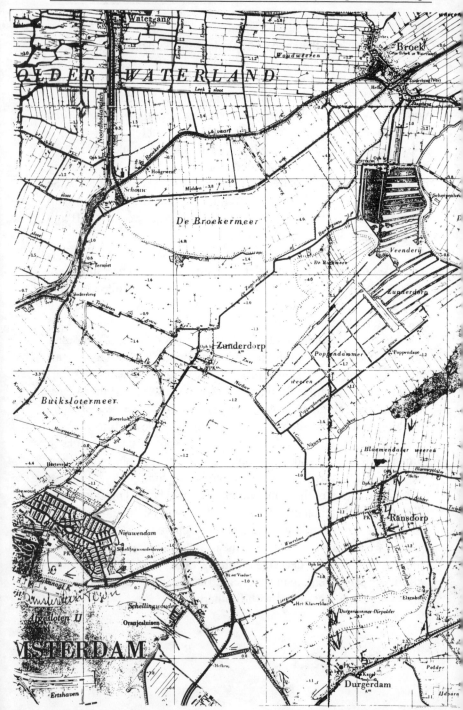

Detailed local map shows landing area and first stops before entering Amsterdam which was only a few kilometers away.

Chapter 3

The Netherlands

My first hours in the Netherlands made two very distinct impressions on me. One was the amount of water surrounding the area; the other was the friendliness of the people and the great numbers who spoke some fair to excellent English.

Soon after dark, the young men returned as promised and rowed me from the island back to the place from which we had left that morning and to the house where I had eaten breakfast. There I had food and was introduced to a man and his wife who would take me to their place in Amsterdam.

For the trip I was provided with a warm coat that had gathered the odors of a cow barn, but covered my flight suit to my thighs, helping me to appear more like a local. My transportation was a bicycle with hand brakes. I knew how to ride a bike well, but this was my first experience with hand brakes. I learned quickly as I rode in the darkness following my guides. Luck was with me as we made our way safely into the city.

At one place my guides slowed to point out a hospital. It seemed that our medium bombers were attempting to knock out a factory in that area but they missed and hit the hospital. "The bombers returned later and got the factory. Good, good!" my new friends remarked. It was a gesture of forgiveness and appreciation all in one expression, with a feeling of sadness for those at the hospital. I was starting to understand something of the hell these people were living in and why they were willing to run the risk of resistance.

To reduce the risk to my helpers, if I should ever be captured, I made no effort to remember their names. And in many cases the names they used were not real anyway. I did recall some, however, and learned still others years later. In this case, my helpers were Mr. and Mrs. J. Rensink who lived at Andoornskeet 21 house, Amsterdam-Noord, Holland. He was a barber, and they lived in a house which seemed to have common walls with those which adjoined it.

Bicycles were not left out at night, so it was natural for all three to be brought inside. My extra bike thus would not be noticed. The next day a man with organizational connections visited. He wanted to be sure I was soon moved to another location, and from him I inquired about my fellow crew members. He told me that everyone except the bombardier had landed safely, but they had all been captured by the Germans. Identified by his dog tags, the bombardier was pronounced dead where he landed. For all but one to be reported safe was encouraging news. However, the official report upon my return to England read as follows:

Position	Rank/Name	Status
Pilot	Capt. John W. Watson	Returned
C.P.	2 Lt. Clayton C. David	Evadee
Nav.	2 Lt. John G. Leverton	P/W
Bomb.	2 Lt. Vance R. Colvin	MIA
R.Op.	S/Sgt. Harry Romaniec	P/W
T.T.G.	Sgt. Eugene R. Stewart	P/W
B.T.G.	Sgt. William H. Fussner	MIA
W.G.	S/Sgt. Samuel L. Rowland	MIA
W.G.	Sgt. Fred H. Booth	MIA
T.G.	Sgt. Roman P. Kosinski	P/W

I have never been able to reconcile the differences, but as I learned years later, only four men were initally taken to a prison in Amsterdam before being moved to their prisoner-of-war camps. These were the four men who were officially reported as POWs. I do not know at what point Sergeants Fussner, Rowland, and Booth were killed, but they were.

I spent two nights and two days with Mr. and Mrs. Rensink before being moved to my next location. But before leaving their house, Mr. Rensink made sure I left with a clean shave, and he gave me a mug and shaving brush which I've never let get away. He was also my guide to my next stop. It was dark but early in the evening when we left his house. We walked to a crowded ferry that had a number of German soldiers on it; but it was the quickest and best way across the large canal. On the other side we had a long walk to the place where I would be staying. Mr. Rensink took his bicycle along to aid in a faster return home, but because I was not riding a bicycle, we both walked alongside his, which was not uncommon.

When we reached my new location, I found we were at a second-floor apartment over a small business shop at a street corner. Mr. Rensink remained for only a few minutes, then said good-bye. In this new location, still in Amsterdam, I remained for 17 days with Miss Betty Glimmerveen, a maiden lady who worked at the Netherland Bank. Her address was 69 Amsteldyke South, overlooking a street and the Amstel Canal. I spent much time observing the people on the street and the traffic on the canal, which gave me an opportunity to try to adopt more of the local behavior.

Miss Glimmerveen went to work each day and returned each evening at a regular time. This meant that it was essential that I be very quiet in my movements during the day, as no one was expected to be there during those hours.

One day, soon after my arrival, Miss Glimmerveen came home with a suit for me that was an excellent fit. She also brought a shirt, a tie, and a topcoat. Someone she knew at work was my size. I now had civilian clothes which would be necessary for traveling when I left. My G.I. shoes were brown and distinctive, but good shoes that fit were even more difficult to get than clothes, and thus I was given black dye for the shoes. Few, if any, men who evaded were better dressed or prepared for walking than I. This was very important to my future.

Miss Glimmerveen was a good cook and I believe she made the best red cabbage I ever tasted. Food was in very short supply, and a single person couldn't just start buying larger quantities, so some arrangements had to be made. To help out, Betty's sister and her son with a farm connection would appear occasionally with produce and wheat among other items. We ground the wheat into flour, from which Miss Glimmerveen would bake bread. It was much better than that which was usually available at the store.

Using electricity would also create some problems. The apartment was on a coin meter which would cause the lights to go out when the amount paid for had been used. It was then necessary to take a flashlight and put more coins or tokens into the meter. There is no doubt that this method is effective in making people aware of the amount of electricity they use and that it causes them to be more conservative.

News was something you naturally longed for. When the air-raid sirens sounded and you heard the planes going over, you always wondered where the target was. Locally, there was little response to the sirens except to make certain that the blackout curtains were tightly drawn. Amsterdam was on the route to German targets for the planes from England, but it was not a target at that time. In an effort to control information, the Germans had confiscated the radios and had equipped apartments with radio systems that permitted the choice of only three stations. These were naturally German controlled stations which provided only the information they wanted to release in the way they wanted it to be released. Hidden in a closet was a radio which would be brought out each evening so that we could listen to the BBC news. At the same time, one of the German controlled stations was played loudly to cover the very distinctive sound of the BBC.

We also would get some information on the nights when Miss Glimmerveen's sister Willy and her young teenage son brought food. The son was able to converse in English and seemed to delight in briefing us. I never did see the boy's father, but I understood that he was part Jewish. He was forced to wear the identifying J badge and work for the Germans at least one day per week. Up to that point he had not been sent to a concentration camp as his wife was not a Jew.

I was told this story about the forced labor that had come from the boy's father:

> They were being forced to help build barracks or housing for the German troops that controlled the area. As they were putting in the sewer lines they would, when not being watched, put plugs in the pipe and then cover it up. The last task in finishing the buildings was the pouring of concrete stoops. The keys were in the doors ready for moving in. As they poured the concrete stoops, the forced labor locked the doors and dropped the keys into the concrete. Once the problem of all locked doors and no keys was solved the Germans moved in only to find that their plumbing didn't work as expected.

This was a simple, but an effective means of harassment that might be called sabotage.

A more fatal type of resistance was reported to occur on occasion in

Amsterdam when German soldiers would try to court the Dutch girls. From time to time some of the unidentified Dutch girls would willingly go for a walk at night with a German soldier along a canal. The next day the soldier's body was fished from the canal.

While I was not a witness to these reported incidents, I can believe them. They exemplify the determination the people of the Netherlands had to make the occupation of their country as difficult as possible for the Germans. However, in the final analysis, the Germans got revenge.

The peace loving people of Holland have directed their conquest for more land toward recovering it from the sea, not toward taking it from other people. But Holland had fought the Germans for five days, 10-15 May 1940, before it was forced to surrender to the mighty German army. To the survivors, surrender didn't mean quitting. They just fought on in a less apparent way. Their resistance, the smallness of their country, and a language that was less of a barrier than in France and Belgium, appeared to combine and provide the Germans an excuse to be very hard on the Dutch people.

How Miss Glimmerveen became involved in helping me is described in the following letter, written by her brother, John Glimmerveen, from his home near Visalia, California. The details are as they knew them.

Visalia - Jan. 22, 1946

Mr. David, Topeka, Kansas U.S.A.

Dear Sir or family,

I have before me a long letter from my sister out of Amsterdam, Holland who asked me to inquire about Clayton C. David 2nd pilot age 26 years and will try to tell you my sister's story about him: Clayton was on a mission to bombard the German city of Brunswijk, the mentioned city was bombarded. However, on the trip back to England via Holland his plane was shot on fire at 15,000 feet altitude. He was 2nd pilot on board with 10 men, all bailed out. Some were taken prisoner, one was drowned. He landed with only a little scratch on his right hand. He buried his uniform and parachute, the Germans were only 1500 to 1800 feet away, however did not see him. This happened on Jan. 11, 1944 close at Durgerdam and Edam, main cheese market of Holland.

He hid till the Germans disappeared, walked to a Dutch farm where he met a farmer by the name, Schouten who had a son who worked at the Netherland Bank where my sister Betty also is employed. Mr. Schouten Sr. did not know what to do because the Germans were going to search the town for the missing fliers who escaped. They were good Christian people and prayed God what to do. You know if the Germans found them guilty of helping the Americans they would have shot the whole family. They hid him in a kind of stable in the field, next morning they searched the house, but never came to his hideout. By dark they got him out and brought him away to another party over river. Those people kept him two days. They could not keep him either so, the man in the bank told my sister in deep secret the story.

My sister who is 45 years old and not married offered him to take care of him. She has a big apartment. The Mr. Schouten Jr. said to my sister do you know if they find him at your place you sure will be shot. She said OK we will do our part, the Americans give their lives for our cause. We will do the same. So Clayton was dressed as a Dutch farmer with a bicycle, somebody also a brave man brought him over on the ferry boat loaded with German soldiers and Dutch people at dark about 7 o'clock. This was Jan. 14, 1944. They brought him through Amsterdam to my sisters place, who took care for him about 17 days. They, my sister Betty and her married sister Willy and her children took care of his food, clothes entertained him. Told him what they know about the war. Also the underground movement helped him.

He stayed home for 17 days and Jan. 31, '44 was smuggled out of Holland and shipped to England. She has never heard from him any more. He promised to write me and also her. He memorized both addresses because it was too dangerous to have any address with him. He got safe in

England because my sister got a visit from two officers
(Dutch and Canadian), who said they were sent from the
combined English and Dutch Governments to thank her
for her brave deed. He sent greetings to my sister. The
officers asked my sister, "How was it possible for you to
feed him because there was not hardly enough for you to
live on, and how could you give him so good clothes? Even
England people did not have any clothes."

Now my question is, does your boy Clayton still live? If
not I thought you would be interested to hear this little
story. Please write me as soon as possible. My sister asked
me to inquire, she is not so good in English correspondence. Receive my greetings.

Yours truly,

J. Glimmerveen
Visalia, Cal.

As it turned out, John Glimmerveen did not have my complete
address and I didn't fully remember his sister's. Therefore, it was
several years before I received the above letter and sent a proper reply
to his sister. Once we got our addresses straight and I was able to get a
letter direct to Miss Glimmerveen, the following letter was received.

Amsterdam, 28 Maart 1951

Dear Mr. Clayton David,

I cannot tell you how glad I was when I received your
letter of the 23rd November last.

All the years since 1944 I have been very desirous to
know if you were alive and to hear something from you. I
did my utmost to get your address but until some weeks
ago all in vain.

I am very glad that all is allright with you, that you now
have a family too, wife and child, so at any rate these are
signs of peace. Under these days I am not prepared to think
disagreeable things, for now I know that all is well with

you, there is sunshine for me. It is a matter of fact that I have given you hospitality on account of Christian being and because I had to do my duty for the sake of freedom, for which you risked your life. Well we had a hard time but you came through and for this moment all is allright.

In my opinion people that lived together some time, every minute with the death before them, grow deeper and deeper in each other's mind and form in future a part of their lives.

I understand, that it must have been for you a very unpleasant thing to be inclined to write me and not to be able to do so on account of not knowing my address.

I have not visited the barber, who you remembered and whose name and address is, Mr. J. Rensink, Andoornskeet 21 house, Amsterdam-Noord, Holland. Please you will also write to your friend Rensink, he shall be very glad that all is allright with you. I send you a photo of my house, that is a remember of Amsterdam.

Good bye Clayton, I hope that you shall write to me and I answer real soon. Many greetings also for your wife and child.

Yours,

M. E. Glimmerveen

I never made it back to Holland while Miss Glimmerveen or Mr. and Mrs. Rensink were still alive, but I understand Miss Glimmerveen married and continued to live in the same apartment. She also worked at the same bank until she retired. To my knowledge, I'm the only airman she or the Rensinks ever hid in their homes.

For me personally, it has been frustrating to try and make contact with people who helped me when I did not know their names and addresses. I believe Miss Glimmerveen's letter expressed that same frustration of not knowing for certain that I had survived and returned home. In the interest of both helpers and the airmen that were helped, the search continues on both sides of the Atlantic.

Above, Clayton and his wife, "Scotty," stand on the dike of the Zuider Zee near where Clayton landed 11 January 1944.

Left: In 1985, "Joke" Folmer stands in front of the entrance to the second floor apartment where bay windows provided a view from the living room.

Miss Glimmerveen in her living room where Clayton hid for 17 days in January 1944.

Chapter 4

Travel by Train

During my first days in the Netherlands, I gave up my escape kit but retained the two benzedrine pills in case they might be needed at some future time. The kits, though compact and equipped for use, were easily identified if I was stopped and searched. Furthermore, the money in the kit was of more use to the people helping me than it was to me.

I wore my dog tags at all times and figured out a way to keep my G.I. watch. When traveling I tied the watch to the draw-strings on my boxer shorts so I would not make the mistake of letting it be seen on my wrist.

In my escape kit were two passport type pictures of me in civilian clothes. The organization of helpers used one of these on identification papers which all people needed to carry. With identification papers, proper attire, and the correct timing, I was prepared to move on after 17 days at Miss Glimmerveen's. My mind churned with the excitement of travel, and I was anxious to get started on the long trip home.

My guide was a young slender man who wore glasses and arrived on schedule. He had me follow him at a safe distance as we walked along the canal toward the train station for my first train ride. Even though I felt mentally and physically prepared for the trip, I almost made a dreadful mistake. In England, in recognition and respect, you saluted and were saluted by people wearing many different uniforms. Saluting therefore, became an instinctive reaction. This day, while walking to the station, we met some German soldiers. Even though I was in civilian clothes and acting the part of a Dutchman, I caught myself starting to salute those uniforms. From that instant on I knew the value of being in conscious control of my behavior at all times. A subconscious reaction could give away your true identity.

My guide and I arrived at the train station without further incident. The tickets had been purchased in advance, and the train was on schedule. We were soon headed for Venlo, Holland. We sat together, but we did not talk. If anything went wrong I would be on my own and not with him, because if captured I would probably become a prisoner of war. I had landed in uniform behind enemy lines, and changing into civilian clothes did not make me a spy. On the other hand, if my guide should be caught helping me, he would become a statistic. The risk was always there, but I wanted very much not to be responsible for the death of a friend if it could be avoided.

The trip, even though it was one of some distance and several short stops, offered very little in the way of scenery. The shades were drawn well before darkness, but anyway I didn't want to appear like a rubber necking tourist. It seemed safest to pretend to be napping as we rode.

It was well after dark when we arrived at Venlo, and for the first time I became aware of a major difference between riding trains in the United States and Europe. Mentally I had prepared myself to expect someone to check for identity papers, and as a result, I was fully prepared for that when we got off the train and started to exit the station. Seeing an armed German guard at the exit was no surprise to me. After all, we were within two miles of the German border. Everyone was moving quickly past the guard and with my identity card in hand I was prepared to do the same. About 12 feet from the guard, in the dim light, I saw that people were turning in their train tickets. They were not being asked for identity cards. In the United States, tickets are collected upon entrance to a train or soon thereafter, but in Europe, the ticket was normally collected at your destination. Not aware of this difference, the matter of my ticket and in which pocket I had put it was something that I had let slip my mind. To delay now while I checked would be certain to call attention to myself, so I decided it was time for quicker and more positive action. I walked boldly past the guard, flashed my identity card like it was a pass and proceeded quickly on and never looked back or wavered in my manner. Apparently in the mind of the German guard, one more official had just passed his station. In reality, this American on his first train ride in Europe had just learned one of the key differences in traveling by train in Europe as in contrast to the United States.

As we walked in darkness from the station, I felt I had been lucky on a very close call. We walked a few blocks and entered a house where I spent the night. Before retiring, I gave my guide the train ticket and he smiled as we both heaved a sigh of relief. This was as far as he took me. Our trip had been a success, but a few weeks later my guide, Tuibro Suis, was arrested and killed. I do not know the details or the circumstances, but it happened to many fine young Dutch men like Suis. It was often done without a trial or any real proof of guilt.

The man who occupied this house in Venlo was I believe a Mr. Jon Hendrikse, a school teacher whose code name was "Ambrosius." During the night, he awakened me from a sound sleep and introduced me to an attractive young girl about 20 years of age who spoke excellent English. Her name was Joke, which is Dutch and pronounced "Yoe-kuh." She was to be my next guide, but at this moment they were to have me answer some questions to help determine for certain that I was an American pilot as I had said. In some way and somewhere there were methods of making intelligence checks. This was probably a good time and place as I would only be there for one night and I was now being moved down the line through their organization's network. They had only a few hours before I would be exposed to other members of the group. Joke's calm and business-like manner let the interview proceed smoothly, and in a few minutes it was completed. She left for the night with assurance that she would return the next day, and she did. When we tried to locate the Hendrikse house in 1983, we found that the area was a shopping center. The houses had been destroyed during bombing raids on the Venlo rail yards during the war.

It was afternoon and a clear day when Joke and I left the house for our walk to the train station and our trip to Maastricht. In the railroad yard were parked some beautiful steel railroad cars that appeared to be special — and they were. I was told that the German military provided for the sexual needs of their men. It seemed that women who became pregnant while performing their assignment of meeting those needs were well provided for. The object was also to glorify the Fuehrer with healthy babies. These women were referred to by the Dutch as the, "Grey Mice." On our way to the station we had walked past a large house with a large yard surrounded by an iron fence where the women were given excellent care and trained to be good Nazi mothers. If it was necessary to move these women by train, even in their final days of pregnancy, these special cars were equipped to meet any need, including hospital room deliveries.

An interesting sidelight to that general activity was used for collecting information by the British Intelligence. Some of the

German pilots carried cards which showed the place and time of having sex and the verification that health measures had been taken. These were commonly referred to as "Nuci Cards." The span of time between that act and their being shot down over England did on occasion assist in establishing the location of the air base from which their mission to bomb England had originated. Such a German air base might then become the target for a counter-attack.

The train was on time and our trip from Venlo to Maastricht seemed easy under the guidance of Joke. No doubt she had made the trip many times, and when she was able to get us in a compartment by ourselves, we had an excellent opportunity to discuss the circumstances that had brought us both to this point in Holland. Most of our trip was made within sight of the German border and she was able to point out places of danger. Traveling arm in arm I thought we looked like any other Dutch couple that might have been on the train. It was during this trip that I learned about the difficult tests that these underground couriers had to pass before they were accepted by the organization. The work was very dangerous and Joke knew this, but she moved with confidence and was able to make others feel that same confidence in her ability. She knew well the ways of the Germans and was blessed with great observational talent.

Upon our arrival in the Maastricht train station, we were met by two men about my own age. One was tall and thin and the other one was shorter. Years later I would learn that their names were Jacques Vrij and Smit. I said good-bye to Joke and became their responsibility.

Before leaving the station with them, I could not help observing something else that was occuring there. A German troop train traveling in the opposite direction to the train we had been on arrived at the same time. On the platform to meet the troop train was a group of young boys in uniform with their musical instruments. The oldest ones appeared to be in their early teens. As the troop train stopped, these boys came to attention in typical military fashion and began to play music which was designed to lift the spirits of the military personnel. I had just been introduced to a segment of the Hitler Youth! This group of boys, considered too young for combat, had already been indoctrinated with Hitler's military ways. They would become combatants for the future, but were being used to make some contribution to the war effort at this very young age. When a man like Hitler could brainwash adults, you must realize how effective he could be in shaping the attitudes of the very young. A whole generation was growing up under the influence of Hitler and his regime with their ways of war.

We left the railroad station without incident, walked down a main street to a bridge, and crossed over the river Maas into the main section of Maastricht. We passed many stores and arrived at a butcher shop. There I was passed to the care of the butcher, and my two guides departed with assurance that they would return at a later date.

I was with the butcher for approximately one week and that time was not without its interesting events. First, the shop was operated by two brothers, Giel and Jen Ummels. Giel, the one I stayed with, lived over the shop. The living room where I stayed was at the front of the building, allowing me to look down on the street below when the drapes were open.

As in the United States at that time, meat was rationed and ration coupons were required. The butcher shop had to collect coupons at the time of sale and then turn them in to the authorities. My host thought it was quite ironic that I spent one day pasting the used coupons into books which he said would be mailed to Hitler. For me it provided a good laugh and something to do with my time.

There was a young girl and a boy in the house. Both were well-mannered and nice to have around. I was surprised when I saw them provided with a small amount of beer to drink in much the same manner we might give a child a Coke. But I came to realize that for them it was a natural drink and not thought of as something served to adults only. Years later I learned that the butchers were uncles of the children. Airmen like myself who passed through that home were also referred to as uncles to satisfy the children's natural curiosity about their visitors. The girl, Betsy, remembers thinking that she certainly had lots of uncles.

One evening Jen, the brother who was part owner of the shop but did not live there, returned from a trip and came in with a very interesting story that was encouraging to me. He had been on a train that day and had seen two German pilots carrying their rolled up parachutes. They had been shot down by American planes. Having parachuted out and landed safely, they were returning to their base by train. They felt beaten and expressed discouragement about the superiority of the American Air Force. While it was good news about German fliers being forced to bail out, I couldn't help thinking that they had an easier and faster way back to base than I.

There at the butcher's in Maastricht, another incident occurred that brought out the reality of life in such a place. Maastricht is located in that very narrow part of Holland which is surrounded by Belgium and Germany. Under normal conditions, trade and personal relationships exist without great concern for borders. The war and German occupation changed most of that, but it could not change everything.

One afternoon the butcher told me he was going to have company and that I should go to a bedroom at the back of the house and hide under the bed. This I did when time for the appointment approached. I soon heard the footsteps of a lady ascending the stairway and going into the living room. The visit was not long and I heard those same footsteps descend the stairway. The butcher quickly appeared in the bedroom and had me follow him back into the living room. It was not yet dark, but the blackout curtains had already been drawn. We went to the side of one of the windows where my host had me peek with him around the edge of the curtain as he pointed to the street below.

What Mr. Ummels showed me was enough to remind me forever of the narrow line that existed between the enemy and the reality of life under the occupation. Very few cars ever moved on the streets because petrol was nearly nonexistent except for the military. There in the street below was parked a black German car with a chauffeur at the wheel and a German officer sitting in the back. We watched as the lady, who had just been the visitor in the very room where we stood, walked across the street and climbed in beside the German officer. I'm uncertain about the true relationship that existed with the butcher, the woman visitor, and the German officer, but this I do know: Germany had just provided the transportation that made it possible for the lady to make a social call on the butcher who was hiding an American pilot. It was a situation the butcher took some satisfaction in pointing out to me.

Because of its geographical location, I feel that Maastricht, more so than any place I had passed through, represented a dilemma that many people of Europe faced during World War II. Personal relationships develop around the happenings of day-to-day activities. Although strong national ties and beliefs exist, they are tempered at times by personal contacts that have a tendency to create a blending of ways. National differences and personal feelings can easily find themselves in conflict in the middle of a war, creating some unusual

situations and at times even straining family relationships. It is small
wonder that some fliers who were unfortunate enough to land in a
crowd when forced to bail out found themselves among those who
would like to help them, as well as some who would have much
preferred to kill them.

The butchers, Giel and Jen Ummels, were arrested by the Germans
in May and they died in separate concentration camps, at Buchenwald
and Oranienburg, later in 1944.

As I noted earlier, when I was on the run behind enemy lines, I tried
not to remember the names of those who helped me or at least only to
remember their first names. Yet even their first names, as we knew
them, were likely to be "code" or "safe" names. In addition, we were
sworn to secrecy about our experiences when we returned. That
classification of our information was not released for many years, all
adding up to a situation that made contacts across the ocean difficult
to impossible. I was extremely well pleased therefore, when I received a letter from Joke. She was also known as "la petite" by the
Belgian underground.

On the train from Venlo to Maastricht I had learned a few things
about Joke, but it was from fellow travelers in Belgium and France
that I learned more about her resistance work. Several of them had
been helped by her and some had hidden for an extended period of
time in her parents' home. After the war, the following letter received
at my parents' home near Topeka, Kansas, was the first news from
Joke.

Leist 16 Sept. 1945

Dear Clayton,

Yesterday I read your report you made about your
"cook's trip" in Holland, Belgium and France, and it gave
me the courage to write you. I am so happy you did return
safely, and I hope found all in good health at home. I did
not know anything about you and the last 50 people I
brought to the South, because the Gestopo caught me in
April (1944) and after I was condemned to death. They
sent me in September to Germany. It was more exciting
than a thriller film and the prolongation lasted till the 6th of

May (1945) when drunken Russians liberated us. But, now I am 2 months at home. I did not know how good it was to have a home where they wait for you.

Do you remember the boy with the spectacles who brought you to Venlo (called Suebro Suis)? The huns shot him down too. Oh it is awful how many people don't return and they are always the best, those who we love the most. But you'll have the same feeling I suppose about your friends in the Airforce.

The tall dark boy, called Jacques, in Maastricht and the little one, are all safe. I don't think I know more people who you knew so, I'll finish and I do hope you'll write again when you have time. So for now my very best wishes to you.

Yours Sincerely,
Joke

Joke's letter didn't reveal her months of anxiety, starvation, and imprisonment with the loss of numerous close friends and thousands of the Dutch underground. She didn't mention that after being in concentration camps from April 1944 until 6 May 1945 it took her and three friends six weeks to get away from a Russian prison camp. Those were some of the things we would learn later.

When I answered Joke's letter, I informed her about my exciting days and months before my return to England. I sent her a picture of my wife and me taken in front of a cabin at Crooked Lake, Michigan. Imagine my surprise in 1982 when she showed my wife and me the picture in a book about the Dutch underground and the fliers they helped during World War II.

In 1954, after having moved several times, it appeared that I would be able to make a trip to Europe, and on 19 May 1954 I wrote to Joke. Several years had passed since our last contact, but she soon replied as follows:

Leiden 4 Juni 1954

Dear Clayton,

What a wonderful idea coming to Europe! Is it holiday

or business or combination, for you must do it now on a quieter way! I looked at the photo you sent me in 1945, are you much changed, and your beautiful wife, and not living any more in Topeka?

Did you write to the other people in Limburg or shall I do for you when you write again when and how long your stay'll be?

No, I did not go back to the Indies. My parents stayed here (they did not want the older generation back) but my brother went, four years all-ready he is in Sumatra.

I finished my study for "juvenile delinquency" and worked till my marriage in 1950 to Ben de Groot, a "marconist" (secret wireless operator) and now assistant-Surgeon here in Leiden.

We are very very happy, with 2 boys ages 3 ½ and 1 ½ and now a third (a boy again I hope) is coming along.

We live in a very interesting old little city in a "hofje" of 1402 (4 little houses, formerly for widows) with a small garden enclosed on 4 sides by normal houses.

We made doors through, so that we live now in all the little 4 houses (1-room and attic) painted and rebuilt and it is very nice now and picturesque.

I have a real guest room, so you stay with us and we'll show you Holland in peace-time.

When you write or see Kenneth Shaver could you give him my very best wishes. He has a 9 year old daughter now? Hoping to hear from you soon.

Respectfully yours,

Joke de Groot-Folmer

Our trip to Europe in 1954 was cancelled and we lost contact again until 1978 when Joke and Jacques Vrij were members of a group of Dutch underground helpers making a visit to five American cities following a short visit in Canada. My wife and I had a marvelous two days with Joke, Jacques, and Letti Vrij in Pittsburgh, Pennsylvania. Later the group went on to Washington, D.C., to receive special recognition and to meet with President Jimmy Carter at the White House.

Joke came back to America in 1982 and attended the Eighth Air Force Historical Society meeting in Cincinnati, Ohio. After the meeting she returned with us for a visit in our home. In 1983 my wife and I finally made our first trip together to England and Western Europe. At that time we visited Joke in her home on the island of Schiermonnikoog, Nederland. It was a wonderful experience, and we visited the place where the Germans had a flak battery on the island from which they fired at us when we flew over during the war. Our trip was cut short by an emergency at home, but Joke did find time to take us to the dike where I had landed near Durgerdam at the outskirts of Amsterdam. In 1985 she helped us pick up the trail at that point so that my wife and I could retrace my escape route from Amsterdam to Gibraltar.

Modesty is a trait often found and admired in individuals who risk so much to help others, and Joke is certainly modest. It has taken much time and a number of meetings for us to learn about some of the key events in her life that are so important to those of us whom she has helped. This national heroine grew up on a Dutch island in Southeast Asia where her father was an administrator in the sugar industry of the colony for the government of Holland. Her mother taught her and her brother a few hours each day for six years. Thus, when the family moved back to Holland at the beginning of 1939, it was difficult for her and her brother to suddenly become a part of the regular and strict school routine. However, at 17, she was attending college in Zeist when the Germans invaded Holland in May 1940. She had just begun to adjust to the wet and cold weather and to accept the flat country-side, when she began to feel the hatred that existed toward the Germans. Some of her friends and classmates were doing things to resist the German occupation. Some of them were shot and others disappeared. It had been rough for Joke, getting used to new habits and life in general in Holland. She missed her childhood environ-ment. But after the events in May, plus the unfriendly treatment of her best girlfriend, a Jew, by a teacher, Joke was changing.

She had begun to feel that she was a real part of Holland and must help Holland. She began to think about why the teacher had been unpleasant to her friend and realized what it meant to be a Jew in a country occupied by Germans. The friend and her family attempted to leave Holland, but they were betrayed. Her friend died later in a concentration camp. In 1941 after her best friend disappeared, Joke went home to Zeist to visit her parents. A family friend asked her to deliver a message for him. She didn't know what it was, but being a sweet young girl it was easy for her to go through the German soldiers and not be questioned. She continued delivering messages unaware that her parents had been hiding students and Jewish people in the house. In their own way, her parents had already been active in the resistance for some time.

The events that had happened around her and the disappearance of her Jewish friend caused Joke to be drawn to the interests of the students who had become active in the resistance in 1940. In 1942 they asked her to do courier work and escort an RAF crew to the south. As the underground saw her successes and as her confidence increased, she became involved in the movement of people. By the time she was arrested on 28 April 1944, she had helped approximately 320 people of which 120 were American, British RAF, and Canadian fliers. The others were civilians as well as military people from Holland, Belgium, and France who needed help. Naturally there were Jews among those she helped and even some Russians. Joke was sometimes called "The Little Rabbit" because she would refer to those she was escorting as rabbits. A contact with another helper in the chain might be, "I have two rabbits. Can you use them?"

During the war the people of Holland hid over 200,000 Jews and anti-Nazi activists from the Germans. Some 1,600 fliers who parachuted from their damaged planes or crash-landed in Holland were helped by the people of Holland. Some of the airmen were later captured by the Germans, but the Dutch people made every effort to help get them back to England. The 120 helped by Joke was the largest number assisted by any of the women who made up the main force of the some 15,000 people of Holland who helped the fliers.

Today Joke knows the names of 72 of those 120 men she once saved and is still in contact with quite a few, their wives and families. But there are many many more she has been unable to locate in the United States, and so the hunt goes on. Joke seeks the satisfaction of knowing that another person she helped was able to return safely to his family.

Joke, like many others, paid a price for the help she provided. On 28 April 1944 she and her mother were having lunch at the Central

Station in Amsterdam when they were both arrested by the Gestapo. Joke and a friend had escorted five British fliers in April 1942. The friend had been arrested and put in prison. Though treated kindly, she had been in solitary confinement for 14 months before she broke and gave Joke's name and address. Joke had changed addresses many times, so the Germans had followed her mother. Always careful to have no material on her, Joke was determined to tell the Germans nothing. They knew only about the first five people she had helped. However, they kept her in solitary for five weeks at Scheveningen prison, then in the Vught concentration camp, and then in the Utrecht prison where she was at the time of her trial. Her mother was in prison for three months. Joke's trial in September was with one of the underground groups of 1942. She was given the death sentence. Then she, with the group, was abruptly transported to Germany, at the time of the battle of Arnhem, where nobody wanted them.

The prisoners were shoved about, and Joke was sent from Anrath to Dusseldorf, to Ziegenhain, to Cottbus, and finally to Waldheim in the Russian zone. Her papers from the trial were lost, which saved her life. The lack of identification papers for the condemned underground workers confused the record-conscious captors to the point of pro-crastination. Joke told me she was one of 300 women from occupied Europe; there were Dutch, French, Belgian, Danish, Norwegian, Finnish, and even Turkish prisoners in those camps. Only 32 survived the many months of confinement and torture. She feels that her good health from much exercise, which began with her years on the island in Southeast Asia, was a key to her survival. She had learned always to keep herself busy and to have a creative imagination. She tried to get the best possible out of every day. She and the others made small things out of scraps of material, and the women in her area sang a lot.

During her 14 months of captivity, Joke hung on to one of her father's linen handkerchiefs and secretly embroidered it with names of the prison camps, bits of songs, and mind-boosting thoughts. She hid the needle under the skin of her palm so that the Germans wouldn't find it, while crushing the handkerchief in her hand and holding it to her nose so that her germ-fearing captors wouldn't take it away. Thread was obtained anywhere and everywhere — sometimes off a barbed wire. Joke told me, "When you know you are condemned to death and every day might be your last, you try to make it the best."

On 6 May 1945 Russians unlocked the doors of the prison and Joke and the other women hid in the men's prison. She said, "The Russian soldiers didn't liberate anything. They were just looking for women, healthy ones, not starved ones like me and my cell-mates who had lost 30 percent of our body weight. We had to steal to get food after the Russians arrived. We thought the Dutch Red Cross trucks would come for us, but they never came."

Joke, two girl friends, and one young man tried to get to the Netherlands, but their weakened condition limited them. So they devised a plan to walk to the Elbe, find a boat, and float out of Germany. After many days hiding, and stealing food, they got to the river and had even found a boat. They were only ten kilometers from the American zone in Dessau and freedom when three Russian soldiers shot at them and forced them to the shore. They were soon led to camp Coswig.

Coswig was only a waiting place for the Russian working camp at Odessa for all the non-Germans without legitimate papers, who were afraid they would never get home. (Several thousand didn't, as the Russians took them to Russia to work rebuilding the countryside and they were too weak from being in prison to survive the hard labor and extended captivity.)

Finally fate stepped in. The American Army found a camp that contained 3,000 Russian prisoners and traded them to the Russians for the 3,000 people in Joke's camp. The Russians made them walk for three days to get to the exchange point and they only had one slice of bread to eat each day. The Americans delivered their well-fed Russians via trucks.

The Americans de-loused Joke and her friends and took them back to Brussels and then to Holland. She arrived home in June, some six weeks after she first thought she had been set free by the Russians at a German prison camp 500 miles away. The Americans had taken them all the way to Brussels before the former prisoners actually felt they were free and the war was history. Death had been so close for so long that they considered themselves fortunate to survive.

In 1946 Joke — Johanna Marie Folmer — was one of seven Dutch underground workers (the only woman) to receive America's Medal of Freedom with the gold palm. She is also the only Dutch woman with the English George Medal. She is one of only three women whose name carries the Netherland's highest military medals "Unmaerkelse," The Bronze Lion. She also received a Croix de Resistance medal from France.

For many years her six children, including two foster children, didn't know of her wartime experiences. "When we did learn, it helped us to know her better," one of them stated. Joke had to retire from her social work position in 1980 because of camp-related illnesses. She reports that many of the people who were in prison camps have never fully recovered. "When you are on the brink of starvation, nerve ends die," she stated, and continued with the observation that "Anger, fear, worry for five years saps one's energy. Nearly everyone has some problem. For many it has come out later in life." The government of Holland recognizes this as a legitimate illness, calls it "War Syndrome" and gives sufferers a pension.

In 1986 when Joke was visiting in our home, I asked her, "How did helping Allied airmen affect your personal life during and after the war?" She replied, "Realizing that *every person counts* (even German guards) and *not systems.* Deep grief (many good friends shot or died in camps and prisons), joy and laughter about small things, and lasting friendships. I need not explain that waiting 11 months to be shot made us look at life differently, glad for every day and nearer to God than ever before."

Jacques Vrij

Jacques Vrij and the other helper, Eugene Smits, met Joke and me at the railroad station in Maastricht, Holland, on or about 1 February 1944. Jacques was arrested by the Germans in May 1944. He survived by escaping from them and went on to live a full and rewarding life dedicated to his family, his church, and his country. He retired as General-Director of Transport of Holland's Ministry of Transport and Public works. From the comments written about him in the 18 February 1974 issue of *Profiel* when he retired, the following information is available.

Mr. Jacques Vrij was born in Emmen, Holland, on 18 April 1916. After finishing an advanced primary school, he went to a teachers' seminary. He obtained his teacher's diploma, his school director's diploma, and a religion diploma. While serving in the military, he was a sergeant in a bicyclist regiment. After the capitulation in 1940, he went to Maastricht to work for the Transport Inspection of the Ministry as adjunct clerk.

Johanna Marie "Joke" Folmer received America's Medal of Freedom with gold palm on 4 September 1946 from Col. Frank Johnson, an American attache at The Hague in the Netherlands.

Kenneth Shaver, Jacques Vrij, Clayton David, and "Joke" Folmer together in 1978 at Pittsburgh, Pennsylvania — their first time together since World War II.

*1982 — "Joke" in the David home, shows Clayton the embroidery work she did on one of her father's handkerchiefs while in prison and concentration camps. Delicate work wove a reminder of each location where she may have been executed. (**Times Leader** photo)*

F. Baron Van Heecberen Van Walien, the chief of the Transport inspection in Maastricht, had this to say about Jacques:

Vrij made a favorable and pleasant impression. He was given the job of working with the rationing of benzine. First as co-worker, then as chief. Everything, all the petrol and oil, at that time was bought with coupons. Vrij did his work well, serious and trustworthy. He was serious but had a sense of humor. You could feel that he lived under heavy stress. He was quick at finding himself in the resistance, the underground. I am convinced he did it because of his religious conviction. He derived much strength from his faith. We knew that he belonged to the resistance, but did not know exactly what he did. He had once brought us some Jews so we knew from experience that he was helping oppressed people. They stayed with us for a couple of days and soon Vrij himself took them across the border. In Belgium they were safer. I didn't want to know anymore about his work. That way I could never say anything.

He was often "ill" or he would ask for a couple of "vacation" days to "visit his family." He would get them of course, but that would put him in a difficult position toward the office. Oh, Vrij isn't he here? Where is he now? I would say then that he was ill and he must be at home. Little by little it was known that he was in the underground. That had to have a bad ending. Around May 1944 I came back at 4:30 from the department. My door was kicked open, there stood a "gentleman" from the S.D. (Security Service against the underground).

Where is Vrij? He works here. He will be arrested immediately. Call him in!

He could be warned, maybe, but I heard that he was arrested. The S.D. had the whole building encircled. We went to his room and there stood Vrij with his hands up. Two men frisked him. Strobel, the chief of the S.D., sat behind the desk. I went to stand close to Vrij. Perhaps he could say something. It did not work. He was grabbed by the collar and literally thrown into a car. They took him to the nearby Wilhelmina prison and kept him a day and a half.

Since we wanted to know how things stood, I went to Strobel and inquired, Mr. Vrij is arrested, when will he be back, because if he is going to be away for a long time we must look for someone else. (I had to say something.) And what has he done? The reply was, "Der Vrij? He will never come back. He will be shot right away!"

Vrij stayed with the S.D. 10 or 12 days. In that time the invasion was awaited and for that reason all the prisoners were taken to the concentration camp in Vught. From that camp he escaped with two others. After the war we, of course, temporarily lost touch. Later, I saw him regularly at meetings at the Ministry in Den Haag. I could hardly figure that strong man who saved so many pilots and Jews. But a few people expressed their greatness in difficult situations.

Some of the danger and difficulties of working in the resistance are expressed in the comments of W. H. Van Keulen, also in *Profiel*. He stated:

We like to talk, but not about the resistance. It still moves me too much. But this I will say about the cooperation with "Leo" who after the war was known as Jacques Vrij. One of the groups that saved pilots was infiltrated with three Dutch S.D.'s. Numerous pilots and a number of resistance fighters should in the end inevitably become the victims of those people. The difficult decision was that the S.D.'s would be lured by the resistance fighter "V" near Sittard. According to what was decided, one of our own members would bring the S.D.'s along the western edge of the Sittard-Roermond railroad line near the small tunnel across from the knit fabric manufacturing plant where the resistance men, Vst, Vrij and myself would be lying in an ambush.

At the moment when the S.D.'s went by the tunnel in question, a peasant with a horse and cart came and hindered us. The plot could not be carried out. We decided

that Vst and I on bicycle would pass one of the S.D.'s on the
way to the other two who were running a bit further. That
way Vrij and V would take care of one of the S.D.'s. The
first eight shots wounded the two S.D.'s and as they tried to
escape one was shot dead. In the meantime, V and Vrij had
also gone on the attack but their shooting missed. The S.D.
fled shooting in the direction of the tunnel and quickly
disappeared. After the encounter, V, Vst, Vrij, and I went
with three bicycles in the direction of Sustern.

Six months after that incident, Jacques Vrij was in prison at Vught.
Sharing much of his captured experience and his escape was P. R.
Raedts, a man who at the time of the article, still carried the scars of
German "treatment." He was a member of the underground force in
Helden-Panningen. He knew Mr. Vrij only superficially when they
saw each other in the Tongerseweg prison in Maastricht. Reports Mr.
Raedts:

From there we were transferred to Wilhelmina prison at
Maastricht. It was a cloister that had been requisitioned by
the Germans. Then one day we were taken from
Maastricht to Vught. After a while we were put to work
taking apart shot-down planes. During that time all was
discussed — escaping was also talked about. We found
ourselves together in barracks 21. More transports were
brought in daily and it became more and more crowded.
We lay in bunks three high. The night of August $^{17}/_{18}$, 1944
is a night I shall never forget. We were working at escaping
because we knew what would happen to us if we stayed.
We were interrogated continually by the S.D. Now they
had found something in the south and then something in
the north.

The Germans were busy installing a railroad line near
the camp. For that reason a temporary gate had been
installed in that area of Vught which was enclosed with
barbed wire. It would be possible eventually to pass under
that gate. Outside of it stood a sentry and further on was a
watchtower with a spotlight.

At 12 o'clock we went through a window. Jacques and I

wore only striped prison pants. We, of course, had no civilian clothes. We had watched a while and then the sentry had been called by his friend in the tower. After that we began to dig through the sand under the gate. The whole time we were on our backs because otherwise we could not see the barbed wire. After we passed under the gate we passed through the woods, and after much meandering we came to a railroad crossing. The railroad guard cautioned us that the commanding officer of the camp lived on the opposite side and that there was a sentry on duty. We asked him for a safe address. No, we did not know him, but we were in luck. He showed us a house alongside the track. We went there and after much knocking a grey haired lady looked out of the window. When she saw our half-naked bodies completely ruined by the barbed wire, she invited us in. "We have escaped — will you help us?" Jacques asked. To the master of the house he said how he could find some clothes. The parents of Jacques lived in Den Bosch, near Vaught. The gentleman got some clothes. Jacques was the first to leave or to be taken away. Afterwards, I dressed myself by putting clothes on over my prison trousers. I still have them. Thanks to Jacques Vrij, our escape succeeded. Mr. C. M. P. Coolen, Principal inspector of transportation in Limburg, commenting on Jacques Vrij said, "After the liberation May 6, 1945, Mr. Vrij came back to Maastricht. He has always been very cautious except in the war. He was always afraid of harming the interests of his brethren. So, he would not willingly say any thing that he would not be responsible for."

While Jacques was head of passenger transportation in Maastricht in 1945, Mr. Coolen noted that, "During the day Vrij was in the office, but in the evening he worked almost exclusively for the underground which was no longer illegal. The next morning he often came to the office with a sleepy head, and some mornings he was a half an hour late. When questioned about this, Jacques replied, 'The office who helped me so much during the war, and those who assisted me I do not abandon. I sense my moral obligation. I shall pay my debt, but when I have paid my debt — perhaps I should go to another job.'"

Mr. Coolen's comments continue, "Mr. Vrij was later transferred to another bureau of transport so he could study law. After four years as part time student, he received his Doctorate in 1954. On February 27, 1963 he became the General Director of Transport for the Netherlands. His co-workers and subordinates saw him as a man in search of excellence in the results expected from his department, a man who wanted the best for the society, and searched for the facts in making decisions." (End of information from *Profiel*.)

Jacques risked his life more than once during the war and risked his career for what he knew was right. Through it all he maintained his sense of humor which has been passed on to his family that consists of his lovely wife, Letti, three daughters, and one son. Jacques has been decorated with the Medal of Freedom, the King's Cross for Courage, Ridder Nederlande Leeuw (Knight Nederlande Lion), and Commandeu Oranje Nassau (Order of Orange Nassau).

Illness forced Jacques to take early retirement, but he is a fighter, and has fought back to live a full and rewarding life exemplifying his great faith and concern for others. Each visit with Jacques and Letti, whether it was in the United States or Holland, has been rewarding and memorable. It was not surprising to hear that in Israel trees are planted bearing his name. A tribute to a Christian gentleman.

When asked why he chose to help 80 aircrew members and also a number of Jewish compatriots, and how it affected his life, Jacques replied, "The helping Allied airmen — and the rescue of Jewish people — does remind me continuously that we have to resist undemocratic forces and that we have to strive for a righteous society with space for all men." He pointed out to us that many of the Jewish families lost to the Netherlands during the war were merchants and small business owners. Their removal from society left a void that delayed the recovery process in Holland, a recovery that has appeared remarkable to an outsider.

Betsy Franssen-Moonen

At the age of 11 was Betsy Franssen-Moonen too young to be a

Picture of Jacques Vrij taken about the time when he was active in the resistance.

Letti and Jacques Vrij pose with Clayton in their home in 1985.

helper? The normal answer would be, "Yes!" But she represents what happened when escaping airmen were hidden with families.

Elizabeth-Johanna Catharina Moonen was living with her uncles, Giel Ummels and Jen Ummels, in Maastricht when I stayed in their living room above their butcher shop the first days of February 1944. In 1950 I received the following letter from her.

December 10th, 1950

Dear Friend,

War is done long since six years; but I'm sure you'll remind that you have been at Maastricht under very bad conditions, but that's over too, so we don't need to talk about it, although we suffered very much by it.

I write this letter on behalf of my two uncles who are dead; both died in a concentration camp. One at Buchenwald and the other at Oranienburg. My uncle asked me to write to you if he didn't come back. But I couldn't execute this commission earlier, for but now, we found your address, this very day. So, I hasten to do it today. I'll not trouble you with this letter, but I confess that I would be very glad to get an answer from you and to know how you are now and what about your job and conditions of life. Do you like it a longer letter from me, next time? I trust you will let me have an answer to the present letter.

With my best greetings, I remain

Yours very truly

Betsy Moonen

Niennestiraat 17-19
(Nieuwstra)
Maastricht, Netherlands

There was a risk to the lives of children as well as adults. However, children could be expected to be a part of the family which was trying to live as normally as possible under German occupation. For us escaping airmen, children and their accepting innocence in the whole situation tended to reduce tensions and permit our minds to wander back to our own childhood with our families. We could think of freedom, open spaces, and family love. We made comparisons that varied in many ways except for the love that we expect in a family.

Children that were old enough to go to school and be with others their age seemed to develop a natural sense of the need for security. In conversation with some of them years after the war, they give accounts of seeing or hearing certain things which were never explained. If, for example, a child told a most trusted friend about resistance efforts occuring at home, it was accepted as a personal secret and never repeated. Learning to live under oppressed conditions seems to develop a type of personal discipline which is not as common in a free and open society.

Betsy was old enough to remember how her father had escaped out a window and over the roofs of buildings to avoid being arrested by the Gestapo. He, too, was active in resisting the Germans, and it was after the war was over that he learned about the fate of Giel and Jen Ummels. Like so many children under German occupation, the meaning of arrest, prison, escape, or death was learned by Betsy at an early age.

During the war children in Europe and Great Britain were reared in the awareness of war and all that goes with it. In the German-occupied countries like Holland, Belgium, and France, the training of children often took very different directions. Although most were being reared in an atmosphere of passive or active resistance designed not to attract attention, there were the public displays of the Hitler Youth Movement which was dedicated to open war in support of Hitler and his beliefs. Many of the active resistance workers and their families have remained reluctant to reveal their experiences. However more of those experiences need to be described so the young people of today can learn the facts from those who were there. In recent years some of the Allied aircrew helpers in Holland have joined with the schools to share their experiences in an effort they hope will keep history from being repeated.

Today Betsy and her husband, Pierre Franssen, live in Venlo, Holland. They have a son, Marcel, who like other young men has accepted his military obligation. Betsy and Pierre own and operate a successful deli and live above the store. Their marriage was arranged and brought the operation of two family-owned butcher shops together. In the arrangement, Pierre agreed to give up his studies as a dentist and operate the combined business. They have not escaped or fought the evolution of change, but have changed with the times and evolved the butcher business into a deli which meets the needs of today's shoppers. Their marriage, their business, and their lives represent a blending of the past to the present and a preparation for the future.

When asked how being around Allied airmen had affected her life during and after the war, Betsy put it all in perspective by saying, "We were glad when all was over — gone, we could speak, sing — we remember, we never forget — and learned at home a discipline that some things are a personal secret."

Clayton with Betsy and her husband Pierre Franssen in 1985.

Betsy Franssen-Moonen provided this 1938 picture of the Ummels and Moonen family. Adults are Aunt Truda Ummels, Giel and Jen Ummels who died in separate concentration camps in 1944, Mother Moonen, and Father Moonen. Front row left is Betsy Moonen and her brother, Mathieu.

Chapter 5

The First Border Crossing

After about one week in Maastricht, my host, the butcher, told me I would be leaving. As promised, Smit, one of the men who had delivered me to this location, returned to start me on another part of my journey. It was dusk as we began our walk through the streets of Maastricht. We went two or three miles before arriving at a street corner where I met my next guide, a girl about 17 or 18 who seemed even younger because she was so short. She was less than five-feet tall, but was strong and in good physical condition. Years later I learned that her name was Marianne Spierings. Her code name was "Cato."

It was dark, and my new guide was riding a bicycle. I certainly felt odd when she told me to get on the back of her bicycle so that she could give me a ride. It would have been more natural for me to be the one pumping and steering the bike. But to be practical, she knew where we were going and I did not.

Crossing the border from one country into another added an extra challenge because these were places where the Germans had guards and natural check-points. Going from Maastricht, Holland, into Belgium could be accomplished by travel over land at certain points or by crossing the river at still other locations. I was moved via the land route.

My identification papers and my own inadequacy made going through a check-point before a German guard a poor risk. The challenge was to get me across the border undetected. My guide, Marianne, quickly rode me the two or three miles toward the border. I don't remember seeing other people along the way, but it was not an isolated street, just dark.

When we were within 100 yards of the border, Marianne stopped, and we both got off the bicycle. She then placed the bicycle into an open shed alongside the road, and we proceeded on foot. We were on the opposite side of the road from the German guard-house, but we could clearly see it. We hid in the shadows as the German guard took his stroll around the outside of his guard-house. When he finally went inside Marianne instructed me to continue along that side of the road, hiding behind a privet hedge which was lower than the roadway. Crouching, I went past the border check-point to some 30 or 40 yards beyond and waited for Marianne as she had instructed. In the meantime, she checked past the guard who knew her and engaged him in some small talk to be certain he would not be observing as I moved through the area.

Years later I learned that via different paths in this area, Marianne had managed to get a total of 72 people across the border into Belgium. Her method of operation also brought her nearly 40 years of scorn by some neighbors and would-be friends who knew only what they saw, which was not as it appeared. Her regular work, as well as helping men like myself, required that she cross the border through this checkpoint often. She decided the only way was to develop a friendship with the German guards to create trust instead of suspicion. To do this she would bring the guards cigarettes and small items and then sit in the guard-house and talk with them. The local people saw this as fraternization with the enemy and treated her accordingly by their actions and gossip.

In her own mind, Marianne had chosen to be a helper for the sake of the individuals involved and not because of any great feeling of nationalism. Although many people do good things for the favorable recognition it brings them, Marianne worked to achieve the results which brought aid to those she helped. Without such helpers, I might not be alive today to write this tribute to those unsung heroes and heroines who risked everything to help downed fliers.

When Marianne again joined me we were out of sight of the German guard. Together we walked a few blocks, and she led me to a house where I would remain while she returned to somehow bring two more fliers across the border.

I doubt that this particular situation of leaving a flier in that home while returning for others happened too often, but this stop of an hour or so made an impression on me. I remember that the lady of the house appeared to be very uncomfortable with my presence. That is understandable when you realize that I was their ticket to death if the Germans had in some way been following us. While I was treated kindly and given something to eat, we remained in the one room where I had entered. The man seemed more relaxed and comfortable with my presence than the lady. I understood she had brothers who had been conscripted and were serving in the German army. I believe that would be cause for mixed feelings, and I've often wondered how we would react in a similar situation. Here was a family faced with the life-threatening condition of my presence while they had family members who were being forced to serve in the army they were hiding me from. How would we go about trying to make the best of a bad situation? I'm pleased that they had been willing to be of assistance on our side. I hope it never brought them any harm.

When Marianne returned with the other two men, we walked a few miles and entered a house at the edge of a village. Here we remained overnight and prepared to move on the next day. It had already been established that Marianne and two of her friends would be taking us by train to Brussels the following day. The friends were attractive young ladies, of about 20 who were thin and approximately five-feet, four inches tall. The three young ladies moved with what appeared to be confidence and determination. They were accepting the challenge like three young cheerleaders leading their team to victory.

To make the trip by train would require money, so the man of the house, who must have been Marianne's father, proceeded to take care of that. From a back room he brought in and opened a briefcase full of small bundles of newly printed bills. I received the impression that the underground in this area had the means of printing, or at least securing, money if and when necessary. Today as I learn more and look back, it doesn't really matter about the source. There was a need for money, and in this case it was available. I guess it was the apparent quantity that surprised me most. The incident provided me the satisfaction of knowing that for the moment at least they had enough money to continue providing help. Train tickets and the many other things necessary required money.

While we three men spent the night on the floor in the house we were informed that there were three other American fliers in a shed back of the house. One of the two men that I arrived at the house with was an American. He had been injured and had previously hid for a few weeks while his injuries improved so that he could travel. The other man was an English flier.

With the three of us in the house, three more in the shed out back, and three girls to act as guides the next day, I had the feeling it was the night before a mission — a mission with the objective being the mass movement of personnel. For the first time I would not be a lone traveler. Before retiring it was proper that we should have some tea. It was good English tea and our host served it with great personal satisfaction. Good tea was difficult, if not nearly impossible, to acquire. Having some to serve us meant they possessed something the Germans didn't think they could possibly have. Little acts like that always seemed to do something for the morale of everyone; at least for me it was something to remember forever, even though I seldom take time for tea.

When we visited Marianne in 1985, we learned that a few months after helping me, she was scheduled to meet a fellow helper who would have men for her to transport across the border. She arrived at the prearranged place at the appointed time, but her contact was not there. She waited for a few minutes to ponder the situation, then aware that there were problems in the organization and many helpers had been arrested, decided this missed contact was a clue to how close the arresting Germans were to her personally. She departed the rendezvous location and without returning home left the area for Northern Holland.

In Northern Holland, Marianne got a job as a nurse's aide and remained there until after the war was over. The various clues she had used to make the decision not to return home that fateful day kept her from being arrested and sent to prison or worse. She learned later that the Germans had gone to her home to arrest her. They would have found her had she returned as expected, and at home, no one knew where she was.

It is now known that one man in a chain of helpers gave names to the Germans in an effort to free his mistress from prison. That information along with the Germans successfully passing one of their men off as an Allied airman, who indeed had been shot down, resulted in the arrest of some 300 helpers. The arrests occurred throughout Holland, Belgium, and France during a period of about two weeks.

After the war was over, Marianne returned home, married, and raised a family, several of whom work together to operate a successful catering service from the home where I had stayed my first night in Belgium near the village of Rekem. When we visited there in 1985, it took a few minutes before I was certain it was the same house. A room had been added to the side of the house where we had entered and left

41 years before. A new building had been constructed at the rear of the house to accommodate the facilities which are used with the catering service.

Betsy and Pierre Franssen, with whom my wife and I were staying at Venlo, had driven us to Marianne Slabbers-Spierings' home. After lunch, the three of them escorted us around Maastricht and over the route I had traveled in 1944. On our way back to her home, Marianne and I walked across the border together for old times sake. She also pointed out some of the other nearby paths she had used to get Allied airmen across the border. In daylight the border area looked the same as I had remembered it in darkness in 1944. The German guards were gone, but the building where they had been was still there, just less obvious. The building with the shed where Marianne had hidden her bicycle was unchanged. The privet hedge was still there, but trimmed lower than I had remembered it. I could stand there and let my mind's eye see the past unfold before us — a safer and more pleasant way to relive it.

In the evening, two of Marianne's sons catered the meal and served each course delightfully to honor their mother and her guests. We were fortunate to have been there on a day when they had not been engaged to cater elsewhere.

We learned that Marianne had once worked for Jacques Vrij at his office as well as in the resistance. She expressed the reason she helped airmen when she said, "You fliers looked down from your formations of airplanes with fear and uncertainty. We looked up at you and saw friends."

Marianne Spierings, "Cato." This picture was taken about the time she was escorting airmen across the Holland-Belgian border.

Left, Marianne Slabbers-Spierings stands with Clayton in 1985 at the border marker. She hid her bicycle in the building in the background and talked to the German guard while Clayton crawled across behind a hedge on the other side of the road in February 1944.

Below, Marianne in front of her home where Clayton and two others stayed one night in 1944 while three other Americans were in the shed behind the house.

Chapter 6

To Brussels and Paris

Early in the morning, we started for the tram which would take us to the train for Brussels. We broke into two groups and began following our guides for a walk of about one mile to the tram station. It went without a hitch, as the girls knew exactly what they were doing and behaved as if they had gone through this before with fewer people.

The ride on the tram and train went without incident, and we arrived at the railroad station in Brussels about noon. The difference between German control in Belgium and the Netherlands was evident. People moved more freely in the Brussels station. We were even approached by individuals selling silk stockings on the black market. (This was an item difficult to find even in the United States at the time.) Our guides acknowledged that almost anything one wanted could be bought in Brussels. I got the feeling that German officials were responding to the cooperative way in which the King had surrendered the country to Hitler.

We left the railroad station and walked a few blocks to a cafe, where we went upstairs to eat as if we were regular customers, but our dining room was isolated from the common dining room.

The man who was to be our next guide met us at this cafe, and after a time the girls left us. We spent most of the afternoon there, and for the first time I was exposed to the unisex restroom. It made a lasting impression on this modest young man, and even today I have not become totally comfortable with many of the European restrooms. In that cafe I had observed both men and women entering and leaving through a door which bore the initials W.C., for water closet. When it became necessary for me to visit that room, it was with some hesitation that I entered and found regular urinals for men along the wall and toward the back of this room two stalls that had doors on them. One was marked WC Messieurs and the other WC Mesdames. I quickly used a urinal and exited with a sigh of relief that no females passed my backside to use the stall while I was in there.

After dark our new guide led us out of the cafe to catch a streetcar. His timing was good and there was no waiting, but the crowd on the streetcar led to some anxious moments for us six fliers. When the streetcar stopped, there was only limited standing room on the rear platform. When our guide shoved us onto the platform, the conductor began asking for money or tickets. Our guide, unable to get on the platform, was actually standing on the step along with other men. His posterior projected out some distance as he hung on to a hand rail. From this precarious position he handed the conductor money and in clear English said, "Give me seven of the best." The conductor returned his change without apparent regard for the English expression. If he understood our guide's remark he showed no surprise. He had collected our fare: that was his job, and he had performed it.

To add to the exciting start, we had gone only about one block when our guide's posterior knocked the globe off a chest-high street light used to designate the standing area for pedestrians waiting to board a streetcar. Uninjured, he laughed as enough people got off so he could pull himself onto the platform. The ride took us to another part of Brussels where we were taken into a large three-story home to remain for several days.

The lady of this house seemed to be functioning under considerable stress. I am not sure she approved of housing so many people at one time. In addition to the six of us, she had two other American fliers and some Dutch resistance personnel in her home. Two of the Dutchmen said they had been involved in blowing up a government building in Den Haag and destroying records to make it more difficult for the Germans to detect faked Dutch identification papers. Such false identification papers were essential to many people under German occupation.

I do not know everything that went on in that house in Brussels, but I had the feeling it was a very active point in the resistance. The house was well maintained as if to provide for businessmen on an extended visit. The lady of the house had a limited amount of food but did her best to meet our needs with the salads she made — and they were tasty. Among those in the resistance who were going and coming were individuals who could make identification papers we could use to pass the customs officers as we went from Belgium into France.

Although I had an I.D. card from Holland that contained a picture from my escape kit, they wanted something better. For taking pictures of fliers at our base in England, the same civilian clothes had been used over and over since essentially all the clothing we had was our uniforms. The Germans had captured enough airmen with escape kits so that they could recognize those same clothes from the pictures that had been made for many airmen.

Without cameras and film for making pictures in private, the resistance personnel turned to their best alternative. To get our pictures in the clothes we were then wearing, they took us to a public photo booth. A young man took two of us to downtown Brussels on a streetcar during the morning after the stores had opened, escorted us into a photo booth in one of the department stores for a quick picture, and returned us by streetcar to our hiding place. The next day I had new identification papers!

While we were in hiding in Brussels, General Rommel returned from North Africa and paraded through the streets of Brussels in a show of strength. Although it made good conversation, we were content to stay hidden and not observe the parade.

In a few days it was time for us to be moving on to Paris. The guide who had moved six of us across Brussels on a streetcar now found himself with eight fliers — seven Americans and one British — to transport to Paris. They decided it was safer to move us in two groups of four each. I went in the second group a few days after the first four evaders had reached Paris.

The method of moving us was the same for both groups, but the first group had the more exciting trip. When they went to the train station in the evening to catch the Berlin-Brussels-Paris train, there was considerable delay. American planes had bombed the railroad in Germany that day. When the train did arrive, it was overcrowded as well as late. The three Americans and the British flier found themselves jammed in with people who might discover their identity. Therefore, when they reached the Belgium-France border and had to get off the train to pass through customs before the train could proceed, the guide made a quick surveillance of the entire train. He found what he decided was a safer place for these fliers to ride. His decision shows the kind of man he was and explains why I consider him the most unforgettable character I have ever met even though I have never learned his name.

This guide was about six feet tall, had dark hair, and spoke fluent English, American style. The story was that he had been born and brought up in the Netherlands and so spoke Dutch. He had lived in Germany and spoke German like a native. He had gone to school in Oklahoma, and it was here that his English took on the American accent. He spoke proper French and Flemish. In addition, he claimed to speak Spanish, but like a foreigner and not like a Spainard. Not knowing the other languages, I can only attest to his ability with English. The stories about this man were that he was in the Dutch Army and was taken prisoner by the Germans. He escaped from the German prison camp and worked his way into Spain where he asked the Dutch Consul's office to send him to England to join the Dutch military there. Because of his languages and personal background, they asked him to return to Holland and become a part of the resistance and escape activities. This is why he was there helping us.

He wore black German boots that he was said to have removed from a German soldier he had killed while performing his duties. He carried himself like a German officer and reportedly used his command of the German language to associate with German officers when he traveled alone. I am sure that it would have been easy to take him for a Gestapo agent in civilian clothes. To do his job it helped to be very versatile and part actor. Acting or not, his behavior convinced me that the stories about this individual could be true. There were many talents and a lot of finesse among those who worked behind enemy lines. I learned to respect them for the work they did and the way they did it, whether assigned or voluntary.

What this guide had found on the train while at the border was a car full of German soldiers. It had not been necessary for them to get off and go through customs. Their car was not crowded, and many of them were taking up two seats to stretch out and sleep. Into this car the guide took the four fliers after they had passed through customs. In German he chastised the soldiers for taking up so much space on an overcrowded train and proceeded to seat the fliers among the German soldiers for the remainder of their night ride to Paris.

While this tactic was a hair-raising experience for the fliers, the successful results demonstrate that it was a good move on the part of the guide. German soldiers were discouraged from talking, especially to strangers, when on any kind of a troop movement for fear they might divulge some military secret. Therefore, the soldiers made no attempt at conversation though civilians in the overcrowded cars certainly would have.

When it came time for my group of four to go to Paris a few nights later, the train was on time and the trip went smoothly. I was carrying a small suitcase containing a pair of work shoes, shirt, trousers, and my shaving equipment — which would be the bare minimum for a worker on leave. My identity papers said I was a deaf and dumb baker working in France. It was easy for customs to check my suitcase, and there were no questions. There was still an odd feeling, though, about being taken through customs and displaying my forged papers.

As I look back I see some factors were in my favor. The able-bodied men had been conscripted for the army or put into forced labor camps. An unusually large percentage of the men traveling may indeed have had some type of physical impairment. Also, some of the people who worked in the customs office sympathized with the resistance movement and actively supported it when they could. In addition, experience had shown our guide and others that this was one way to move quickly across the border from Belgium to France. However, my discussion with other evadees convinces me that my trip through customs when passing from Belgium to France was a rare experience. Most men were passed over the border at a place and time where they were not seen.

It was about 7:00 am and daylight when we arrived in the railroad station at Paris. As we walked out through the station to a subway entrance, I felt very uncomfortable. At the station, I could see a number of places that I would consider excellent observation points for someone wanting to look down on the travelers in hopes of spotting groups like ours, but apparently, we were not as obvious as I felt because we were not stopped and proceeded to the subway without a problem. At least we had arrived in Paris, an expected stop on our way to Spain.

Chapter 7

Paris

Like many Americans, I had always dreamed of seeing Paris. How I wished this could have been a sight-seeing tour instead of an escape route. But the many German guards and French gendarmes at the railroad station served as a reminder of our precarious situation. We were not comfortable in their presence, and I felt relieved as we left the station and entered the subway. I did not realize at the time how easily we could have been trapped and captured while in the subway. However, we were lucky, and the rapid travel of the Metro soon had us at our destination. We emerged to street level at a quiet and nearly deserted place in the city.

Later we learned how forturnate our timing had been. While we were making our successful arrival in Paris and taking a ride on the Metro, other things were just beginning to happen. Less than 30 minutes after we had left the subway station, a strict guard was placed on each station, and the people were all required to show their identity cards. That could have meant capture for us if we had arrived 30 or 45 minutes later.

After leaving the subway station, we walked a few blocks and entered a schoolyard. The schoolyard was fenced and there were teachers, classrooms and students, but other elements made this school different. In addition to the housing for the custodian of the school, his wife, and daughter, I also suspected that there was space or refuge available for those who needed it. In some ways this place resembled a boarding school with the custodian and his wife as guardians and a devoted priest as the overseer. School was not yet in session when we entered the main building and were escorted down a hall that echoed every step we took. We went down a stairway to the basement and then further down into the furnace room which also contained an electric generator. As we approached what was to be our hiding place, we found ourselves weaving around massive pieces of equipment and entering an area that was seldom visited.

By this time, our original guide had vanished. The custodian had taken over, and close behind him was the priest. They seemed concerned about the number of us gathering there. We would bring the total to nine. In addition to the four of us who had just arrived and the four fliers who had arrived a few days earlier, there was also a Dutchman.

We had just reached the area where the other five were hidden when the custodian was notified that he had visitors. He and the priest would return to the entrance of the building, and we were to remain very quiet. In silence we waited for what seemed like an hour when in reality it was probably ten or fifteen minutes. A lump came into my throat as I heard footsteps in the hall above us, for it was the loud and sharp echo of military boots. The sound stopped at the steel door about ten stair steps above us, and there was an effort to open the door. But the door was locked, and on the hall side of it was a sign indicating that there was danger from high voltage on our side. The German and Vichy French police who had just tried the locked door had no idea how close they were to people they would have loved to find, or they would have demanded that the door be unlocked. The police walked away from the door as rapidly as they had approached it.

When they were gone, the British flier, who spoke French, told us about the conversation that had occurred in the hall above us and emphasized how close we were to being caught. In a few minutes, the custodian appeared and was very excited. The priest was with him and was trying to quiet him down. But why shouldn't he be scared? A wall and a locked steel door were all that had stood between him and certain death a few minutes before. For us there was danger, but probably prison instead of death if we were found. After a brief conversation with the priest, custodian, and our British flier, the British flier turned to us and said, "We are to be moved from here at once. To this school the police have traced a typewriter that was used in making fake passports and false papers. They are not sure it may be the work of a student, but until they know more, the police may be expected to return anytime for a closer search."

"Where are the police now?" we asked.

"They have left the building unhappy with their findings," he continued. "But they are certain to return. The priest is going to lead us to a place in his nearby church. It is a part which has been condemned and is not in use."

We quickly gathered up the items we had and followed the priest while the custodian remained behind to clear away any evidence that we had been in his building. We followed the priest who was tall, thin, and elderly. He was firm in his convictions that freedom and Christianity must live. Walking quickly he led us out a passageway, up through the school building, out a window, across a rooftop hidden from view, and into the old part of the church he had told us about. We climbed a spiral stairway which took us to the top floor of this building, four stories above the street. The priest then turned and quickly walked away, for he had work to do in offering guidance to the custodian and his family so that they would all be calm if and when the police returned. The police did return later in the day and searched the spot where we had been behind the steel door but found nothing. The earlier decision to move us had been a good one!

Our new hiding place was without heat — quite a contrast to the warm area we had just left. It consisted of two rooms with a toilet and wash basin in a small room between the two where we stayed. It was a cold February. However, there was warmth in our hearts and in the eyes of the priest when about 2:00 pm each day, he brought us some food prepared by the school custodian's wife and daughter in their living quarters at the school.

We kept warm by huddling together in groups of four or five with a straw tick on the floor under us and some blankets over us. We were concerned about the need for exercise because we knew that getting into Spain, our ultimate objective, would require a difficult walk and climb across the Pyrenees mountains. Any exercise had to be done without making noise because there were nine of us where no one was supposed to be. We found that push-ups, leg stretches, sit-ups, and lying on our back doing the bicycle with our legs were a few things we could do quietly. The exercises were also helpful in keeping warm.

There was plenty of time for us to learn something about each other, and here is a summary of what I learned: The Englishman, Flight Officer Smith, was a navigator on a British bomber and had been forced to parachute out at night. His civilian job was as a certified public accountant in Brazil working primarily with British firms. He spoke Spanish and French and was the only flier among us who spoke more languages than English. He had returned to England on his own because of the war and joined the British Air Force. One of the American fliers, Lieutenant Donald C. Schumann, was with

Flight Officer Smith when the three of us met near Maastricht. He was the one who had been burned when he bailed out. The underground people had hidden him in a cave and nursed him back to traveling health.

The Dutchman spoke some French and had friends near Paris where he would go once in a while as we all waited for our chance to get to Spain.

William Lock was the pilot of a B-17, and traveling with him was Charles Mullins, one of his waist gunners. Their plane was on fire when they bailed out over Holland. Before Charles got out, a wing came off the plane, and it began rolling. He had crawled to the waist door and been thrown back by the force of the plane's roll when his parachute was accidently opened, and sucked out of the airplane, pulling him with it.

The other three men were from the same crew. They were William J. Koenig, the copilot; Kenneth D. Shaver, engineer; and John R. Buckner, a waist gunner. Their B-17 had crash-landed in Holland on 5 November 1943. They had been immediately captured by the Germans, and a few days later eight of them were being escorted by four German guards to Germany on a train. The guards did not speak English, so these men conceived the idea of trying to escape from the train while it was still in Holland. They had talked about it openly to each other. As they talked, they saw a number of the people on the car they were in leave it and move into other cars. These were no doubt Dutch people who understood English and wanted to be in a safer place where they could not become witnesses. When all conditions including speed and location of the train had seemed right, the Americans had jumped their guards and overpowered them. After disarming the guards and at least knocking them out, the American fliers had jumped off the train. These three had succeeded in getting away with help from the Dutch resistance. Joke Folmer's father had hidden them in his house for several weeks until the Dutch had felt it was safe to risk moving them. Now they were as far as Paris with the rest of us.

After about two weeks in Paris we were all getting restless. The prolonged confinement was not only a cause of restlessness but an indication that something was wrong down the line toward Spain. If things had progressed as we had expected, we could have been in the Pyrenees by now. There was a feeling among us that the longer we stayed in one place with this many men, the greater the risk of being found.

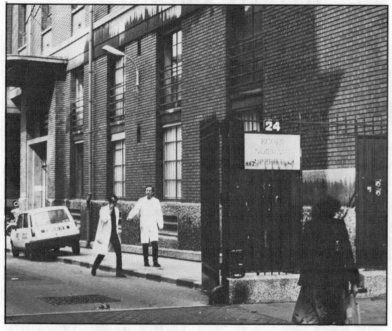

1985 picture of the School (Ecole Normale) at 24, rue Lhomond in Paris, where we were hidden in the basement of the building to the rear. The vehicle gate was closed and we entered through the pedestrian gate next to the building. The custodian, his wife, and daughter lived in a first floor apartment where curtains hang at the windows.

Chapter 8

Arrests and Escape

On this day, 26 February 1944, it was nearly two hours past the time when the priest, Father Superior, usually brought our food, and we had heard nothing. Suddenly there were hurried footsteps and a light knock at the door before it was opened by a younger priest whom we had not seen before. He looked shocked to find so many men in this area. The Dutchman had gone to the country for the day, but there were still eight of us.

This priest did not speak English, so his conversation took place with our British friend who spoke French. We were informed that we must immediately get out because the police were arresting Father Superior at that very moment. The charge for the arrest was possession of black market food, food he had been securing to feed us. If the police found us, it would be prison for us and death for Father Superior and any others who could be identified as helping us.

The situation required immediate action, and yet we did not want to walk out on the only connection we had with the organization that expected to get us to Spain. We selected Flight Officer Smith to go into the street and next door to see if it might be possible for us to move back into the basement of the school. He not only spoke French, but he and three of the Americans had enjoyed Sunday dinner with the custodian, his wife and teenage daughter in their quarters before the last four of us had arrived. That had been possible because Sunday was a normally quiet day when students were not around.

Smith accepted the assignment and used good judgement in the way he carried it out. He returned quickly and gave us this report. Instead of walking into the closed schoolyard and approaching the door to their living quarters, he had decided to walk by and first survey the surroundings. As he did, his eyes caught those of the custodian's daughter, standing at the window facing the street. She recognized him and with a slight hand gesture motioned for him to move on. The police were at the door at that very moment arresting her mother and father. After arresting Father Superior, they had turned immediately to the custodian and his wife with the same charge, possession of black market food.

Now it was clear that we had to move from that location and away from those who had helped us so much. Our capture would probably bring death to our helpers.

We had realized, while Smith was checking out the school next door, that we would need to break up, and we decided then to break into four pairs. The pairing came easy for the pilot Lock and his waist gunner, Mullins. It was also natural that Flight Officer Smith and Lieutenant Schumann, who had been together when they entered Belgium, would stay together. The trio of Koening, Butler and Shaver, who had been through much together, must now have one man shift and join me. Ken Shaver came and asked about traveling with me. Naturally, I answered, "Yes." A few moments later, Butler also came and asked me to be his partner, but I told him Ken and I had agreed we would travel together.

Each pair of men would be responsible for themselves, where they went, and how. Then I heard Koening comment that he would like it if he and Butler followed some distance behind Smith and Schumann. I am sure he thought there could be some help and security in Smith's ability to speak French.

When we left our hide-out two by two, the priest who had come to warn us escorted us into the church sanctuary by way of a side door and out the front door into the street. As we walked through the sanctuary, I noticed several people in there who had apparently entered to pray. I am sure they must have noticed us, and I prayed silently that we would all be free and safe. This was the last time Ken and I saw any of our group of eight while behind enemy lines. We now became two fliers traveling alone in a country we did not know and among people who spoke a language we did not understand.

The young priest's view of that day and the results were explained in the following letter.

CONGREGATION   Paris, Le 5 Juin 1946
     DU
SAINT-ESPRIT

30, rue Lhomond - Paris VS

Dear Sir:

I was very glad to hear from your news and to know by
the same occasion that you succeeded to land safely in
England in May 1944. I also am back again (since June 45)
from my captivity in Germany.

I am the young religious who, on the 26th of February
1944, made you escape out of the Seminary (30, rue
Lhomond) in Paris. One hour after your departure the
Gestapo came in arms with the Dutch Brother (Rufus) to
fetch you. They went upstairs and, of course, found the
nest empty. Raging they came down and wanted to kill all
of us. Finally they took Father Superior, Brother Rufus and
myself as prisoners. The doorkeeper of the "Ecole Normale" and her husband were also arrested.

After three months staying in the prison of Fresnes, the
military court condemned us and we were sent to Neuengamme (camp de concentration) in Germany. What we
had to suffer in that camp you easily may imagine. Father
Superior died in December 44 of hunger and ill using. The
husband of the doorkeeper of the Ecole Normale died there
also.

We, who by God's grace and special protection of His
Providence, are back again, recovered little by little our
health and are quite well now.

I am glad to know that you arrived safe and sound in
America. May God's blessing be with you for ever.

I send you my best greetings and remain,

Yours truly

Robo Mathurin

The sun was shining when Ken and I entered the street, and we took
a southerly direction. We were determined to walk as far and as
quickly as we could without appearing to be fugitives and thus more
noticeable. The streets were quiet but not abandoned. We had not
gone far when we chose a moment to stop and soak in the view we had
of Paris. We could see the upper part of the Eiffel Tower and lamented

the fact that we had passed through Paris without being able to visit it. We saw the tables and chairs which are a trademark of the sidewalk cafes, but they were scarcely used at the time because of the war and the cool temperatures. We saw enough so that it was easy to visualize what the scene could have been at another time when there was no war and the weather was warm. I tried to match what we were seeing with the picture I had in my mind from the travel brochures I had seen about Paris.

It is not easy to walk out of and away from a city as big as Paris, but we felt we had no other choice. Physically we thought we were up to the challenge, and we pressed on. With the afternoon sun on our right, we kept up a fast pace to the south, even though it was impossible always to go in a straight line since we followed the streets and roads the best we could. More than once we were tempted to stop and seek a friendly contact. The greatest temptation came when we were walking across some small plots of farming ground that contained several structures which looked like shelters from the weather for people who worked the land. We saw a few people working there, and I liked to think they were reaching out to us, perhaps with an offer to hide us in one of those shelters; but the risk of identifying ourselves and asking for help, while still so close to Paris, caused us to keep walking. I have since wondered if we walked right by the help we were seeking. I guess we will never know. We were making good time and kept on going.

As the sun began to set, we had walked out of Paris, put some farm land between us and the city, and covered enough distance to separate us from the location where we had been hiding for two weeks. Our feet and legs started to ache from walking after our inactivity of the past, but the adrenaline was flowing in our bodies, and it helped us to overcome our discomfort. At least the air of the countryside was refreshing. Because we wanted to put as many kilometers as possible between ourselves and the hiding spot of a few hours before, we decided to keep walking until after dark. However, we knew we should stop before the curfew hour.

The time to stop seemed right when we entered the edge of a village some time after dark. At least we thought we could risk a contact for help without being exposed to more than the people of the house where we knocked. Something drew us to a house that was not isolated and yet not a standout from those surrounding it. We went up a few steps onto a porch and knocked at the front door. On the street, no one was in sight. The door opened, and a lady appeared, standing in the dimly lit entrance hall. I am sure many thoughts raced through her mind as we used the words "Americans," "pilots," and "parachutes." We were also using gestures to indicate we had been shot down and needed food and a place to stay.

Directing her two young children, a boy and a girl, back into one of the rooms from which they had emerged to view the commotion, the lady invited us in. We had succeeded in the first step to sell ourselves. We had gotten in the door. Luck was with us, and the lady seemed to be taking the situation in stride. Once we were inside, she informed us that her brother also lived there and commuted to work in Paris. He was expected to arrive at any moment but was later than usual since this was Saturday night.

The lady gave us something to eat and waited for her brother before making a decision on what they would do about us. The wait for her brother was not long. When he arrived, they quickly decided to let us stay one night. During the evening, we learned that the lady's husband was an officer in the French Army who had been captured by the Germans and was in a prisoner of war camp. We felt that our blind faith had led us to some wonderful people who saw helping us as one way of doing something to even the score with the Germans. When they used a map to show us our location, we were surprised to learn that we had walked between 20 and 25 kilometers before arriving there.

The lady and her brother were naturally interested in knowing where Ken and I wanted to go. Although they did not seem to have any connections with the resistance, they were willing to buy us train tickets and get us started on the way to Toulouse, which we had indicated was our destination.

It felt good to get our shoes off and be able to rest. We slept with our clothes on as we had been doing for several weeks, ready to make a quick exit. Ken and I shared a studio couch, and even though it was very crowded, it was more comfortable than the floor we had slept on the past two weeks. And the house was warm.

The next morning we were told there was an afternoon train for Toulouse and that they were getting us tickets for the trip. The lady and two of her girl friends planned to walk us to the station and see us off. For two men with no money and sore feet, this was music to our ears. The first day and night on our own could not have gone better. We had put distance between us and Paris, and if we got on a train, we could go even faster.

I have never learned the name of the lady and her brother who kept us overnight, or the exact location of that house, but it was somewhere in or near Brétigny.

Father Robo Mathurin, in his letter of 5 June 1946, informed me about the fate of Father Superior and the custodian of the school. The lady doorkeeper of the school survived her stay in the concentration camp, but died soon after the war suffering from the camp's effects on her health. When I returned to the church and school in 1985, I saw a plaque which recognized that Father Superior and the custodian had paid with their lives for their efforts to help the resistance.

On my return visit, I also learned that the places where we had been hidden were part of other facilities with many entrances and exits which comprised most of a city block. The physical layout had made it difficult for the police to catch people there during the war, so the area was used temporarily by a number of people who were trying to avoid arrest.

When Father Gerand Robo was awarded his "Legion D'Honneur" from The Community of Croix-Valmer, for his participation in the Resistance, he was called a hero of faithfulness to his job as keeper in the main home, Mere des Spiritains, rue Lhomond in Paris. At the awards ceremony, Father Didailler said, "A door-keeper because of his job may have instant surprises, some pleasant, some quite unpleasant, unkind, sometimes cruel; that was the case when brother Gerand (26 February 1944) was told he was arrested and had to immediately follow the policemen who were addressing him. His job almost cost him his life, but all the fliers (and there were dozens and dozens) managed to go through or escape."

With the attitude, "Father forgive them, they know not what they do," Father Robo returned after the war was over from the Neuengamme concentration camp in Germany, where he had been confined for one year, to his assignment in Paris. He continued to serve his church in Paris and other locations in France until he retired. During his final years he was at Abbaye Notre-Dame, Langonnet, France, near Lorient in the department of Brittany, in his beautiful homeland. There he died in December 1985 at the age of 75. In his years of service to his fellow man, the events of the war in particular caused him to bear a heavy burden. I am grateful for his quick action at that critical time in Paris.

Robo Mathurin, door-keeper at the Congregation Du Saint-Espirit 30, rue Lhomond, Paris.

Right, Clayton stands outside the church doors from which they exited in 1944 to avoid capture.

Below, the top windows of this church building are windows to the rooms where Robo Mathurin found eight airmen hiding when he came to tell them they must leave as Father Superior and others were being arrested.

Chapter 9

Traveling Alone on French Trains

It was mid-afternoon on Sunday when the three ladies walked us to the Brétigny train station, gave us tickets for Toulouse, and kissed us good-bye. When the train stopped, Ken and I were waiting beside the tracks and our benefactors were watching us from outside the station fence. This was our first train ride without the benefit of a guide, but we boarded the nearest car like a couple of seasoned travelers. We knew not to worry about giving a conductor our tickets. After all, I had learned in Holland that you turned the tickets in at your destination.

We sat down in a car that was not overly crowded and began thinking about a long ride to Toulouse. That was our destination, clearly marked on the tickets. The train left Brétigny and rolled along to the next stop at Étampes. After some switching, we were soon moving again. The sun was beginning to set, and we realized we were moving west instead of south as we had expected. We took a closer look at the train and saw that it was much shorter than it had been when we had gotten on at Brétigny. Though we were starting to feel some concern, we were not yet ready to abandon this train when it came to a halt and the remaining passengers got off and left us alone in the car.

Now it was time to try and get some information. Pretending to be a deaf-mute, Ken walked over to a trainman who was still on the car and displayed his ticket marked for Toulouse. Ken also pointed to the front of the car in a questioning manner to ask if this car was going on to Toulouse. The trainman shook his head "no" and pointed to the direction from which we had come, then indicated that we should stay on the car. We were at the end of the line, and the train would be going right back to a junction where we could catch a train for Toulouse. For that train we would have to wait until the next day. We weighed our alternatives and followed the trainman's directions.

We never will know if the trainman had guessed our identity and was using a low-risk method of helping us or if he thought we really were as dumb as we acted. Regardless of his thoughts, he ignored us as the car began its return run with fewer than six of us on it.

It was totally dark when the train finally stopped with all indications that it was being parked for the night. We left the train knowing we were back near where we had started, and we were determined not to expose ourselves by exiting through the station with tickets reading Toulouse and no money to replace them.

We took advantage of the rail yard's darkness and proceeded to a remote area where we found a fence. Without hesitation, we jumped over the fence and soon found ourselves on a road leading out of the village. We did not want to be too far from the station, and it would soon be curfew time, so our eyes began searching for a house we might try to get into for the night. We were looking at a large house when the comments from an escape briefing came to mind: "The Germans often take over the large houses for use by their personnel. Therefore, it is best to avoid the larger houses." This we did and walked on about 300 yards to a smaller house with a fenced-in yard.

We entered through a gate and walked down the sidewalk to the front door. When we knocked on the front door, it did not open, but we could hear movement and a door opening in the rear. We turned to the corner of the house and came face to face with a man and his son. Our efforts to identify ourselves and indicate our need for help soon evoked discussion between the man and his son. It was evident that the man saw great risk in taking us in, while the son wanted them to take the risk. I believe the father soon decided it might be safer to take us in than to continue the discussion where we were. They led us to the back door and into the house.

Once inside, we showed our train tickets and tried to explain how we had gotten into the wrong car. They understood and confirmed that there was only one train per day to Toulouse, the afternoon train we had just left. While they gave us food and said we could stay the night with them, they also explained the dilemma they were faced with. It centered around the fact that German officers who were attached to the nearby Brétigny air base occupied the large house we had passed before knocking on their door.

We were in the home of Mr. and Mrs. Gabriel Guillon. Mr. Guillon farmed, and Mrs. Guillon was working away from the home during the day. The son George, who was 17 years old, was attending school. Grateful for their hospitality, we slept with our clothes on, ready for a quick exit.

Ken and I kept a low profile the next morning while Mrs. Guillon left for work and George went to school. Sitting at the kitchen table that morning, Mr. Guillon informed us he would walk us to the train station in the afternoon to start again our trip to Toulouse. He also attempted to teach us how to select the correct car on the train and where we would have to make transfers.

The night before, while we were all five together, Mrs. Guillon had had us write our names and home addresses on small pieces of paper. She wanted to know whom they were risking their lives for, but she wanted that information where it was least likely to be found. We watched as she rolled back a corner of the dining room rug, placed the pieces of paper on the floor and laid the rug back down. When Mr. Guillon decided it was time for us to leave for the train and we walked out the door behind him, I felt we were leaving our mark behind in safe keeping. Certainly it was safer for them to have our names than it was for us to have their names on paper.

When Kenneth Shaver returned to France in 1972 and visited the Guillons, Mrs. Guillon retrieved those pieces of paper from that same hiding place and showed them to him. She also told of the fear she had experienced on her way to work the morning she left us in their home with her husband. That day, people on the bus had talked about two American fliers that were being hunted. A few days later, they learned that two other men had bailed out in the area and that we were not the ones they had been seeking. Nevertheless, it had created some very anxious days for the Guillons.

Even though we did not see any activity at the house occupied by the Germans, we left the Guillon home away from their possible view. We also walked down the road in the opposite direction from which we had arrived the night before. This meant we took a longer but safer route to the station. Before leaving the house, we had agreed to follow some distance behind Mr. Guillon with no contact to be made at the railroad station. We had our tickets, and if we were stopped or arrested, we would be strictly on our own.

The route Mr. Guillon had selected was good, and his timing correct. We arrived at the station with enough time to look the situation over, but with no time to waste. The train was on schedule, and as it stopped we were quick to look for and get on a car marked Orleans, just as Mr. Guillon had instructed. In Orleans we would have to get out of that car and wait several hours for a train with cars marked for Toulouse. As we made it past Étampes, where we had gone in the wrong direction the day before, we started to gain confidence in our ability to travel alone. We soon found, however that we had more to learn.

It was still daylight when we arrived in the station at Orleans. This was a larger station with a waiting room built to accommodate about 100 people. Knowing we had several hours to wait, we strolled around on the platform, checked out the unisex restroom, and looked for an escape route in case we needed one. We wanted to avoid getting into a place with no easy exits and to avoid going through a gate where we would have to show or give up our tickets.

As darkness fell, we were forced more and more into the main waiting room of the station to avoid being too noticeable. A few German soldiers were going and coming, but they seemed to be concerned with themselves and not us. It was a long and precarious wait, so Ken and I separated much of the time, hoping we would be less noticeable alone than together. We also figured that by watching in more directions, we would increase the chances for one of us to get away if a crisis developed.

The curfew hour arrived, and we were still waiting. Now we had to stay in the waiting room because only there did people have the right to stay while waiting for a train. To wait elsewhere was to break curfew and be liable to arrest. With several of us in the waiting room, I saw a policeman enter the door and start checking each person. My first thought was that this must be a check for identity papers. While I still had the I.D. card I had used to go through customs from Belgium to France, I was in no way certain it would pass inspection at this point in France.

As the policeman moved from one person to the next and came ever closer, I began looking for some way to avoid him. I felt trapped, and actually considered getting out of the room. But I decided to sit tight and see what would happen. He was going to reach me before he would get to Ken, so we would not both be checked at the same time. Finally, he was checking people only about ten feet away. It was then that I was able to observe he was checking train tickets to see if the destination on our ticket warranted our being in the station past curfew. My level of anxiety lessened as he checked my ticket and moved on. Ken was watching very closely, and there was an expression of relief on his face when he saw that I had passed inspection.

Soon after that scare, the train we were waiting for pulled into the station. We went out to the platform where we could select our car and get on board for Toulouse. Then the blackout, which had been so helpful to us the night before when we had left the Brétigny station by jumping over the fence, became a real handicap to us. As we walked up and down on the station platform, it was too dark to see the destination name on any of the cars. Since we could not ask directions, we went with the crowd into a car. We could only hope that they too were going to Toulouse.

There were not enough seats for all of the passengers, and as the train pulled out of the station, we were standing along with several other people. After a few hours there was some switching of the railroad cars and we knew the make-up of the train had changed. However, it was still too crowded in our car for us to sit down. By this time, we had become less certain about the destination of the car we were on, but we stayed on it and hoped for the best.

As the night passed, we surveyed the passengers on the train and saw no German soldiers, so we concluded that the train was not taking us toward the coast or to Germany, the two places we were certain we wanted to avoid. When the train began going slowly between stops of short duration, we concluded that we must be in mountainous country. When we were able to get onto the platform between two cars, we could see that we were indeed in mountains, and that it was snowing very hard. Several inches of snow already lay on the ground.

Unfamiliar with the topography of all of France, Ken and I began to wonder if these mountains could be the foothills of the Alps. If they were, our future was very uncertain. We whispered to each other and discussed our choices as we stood there between the cars and away from the other passengers. Ken might have killed a German guard when he escaped from them on the train in Holland. My dog tags were around my neck, and they could serve to help me if we were captured. But Ken had no dog tags. They were in the pocket of his leather flight jacket, which he had left on the train in Holland during his escape. Since we were traveling together, we might both be expected to suffer the same uncertain fate if we were captured. With these thoughts in mind, and seeing no German soldiers or police on this train, we decided to ride it as long as we could. We also determined that if we should be cornered, we would not accept capture if there was the slightest chance for escape.

About daylight, a couple of men noticed our weariness and offered us their seats in a compartment. We accepted their offer and sat for an hour or so. However, we did not feel secure in a compartment with only one exit and traded back with them. We wanted to be on our feet near the end of the car.

As morning progressed, and the train continued on, the rural mountain area under a heavy accumulation of snow appeared more tranquil and less threatening. But we still did not know where we were, and there was no safe way of finding out. As we looked over the car more closely in the daylight, we concluded that, uncomfortable as we had been, this was actually a car for passengers with first class tickets. Our tickets called for second class.

About noon, the train stopped at a station which was isolated in the mountains with a few farmsteads nearby. We could see no village, and only a very few passengers got off or on the train at this stop. When the train started up again, the conductor began to move about, so we went to the back of our car, the last one on the train. It was an uphill pull out of the station, so the start was slow. When the conductor started to check or take up the tickets, we decided it was time to jump off and let the train leave without us. As we hit the ground and walked toward the station, we realized that the passengers who had gotten off the train had already left the area, and that the station agent was alone. He did see us, and when we hesitated about leaving through the station where the other passengers had passed and turned in their tickets, he entered his office.

We did not know if he was going to make a call to the police or if he was offering us a chance to move from his view. We did know we were not at Toulouse and therefore, that our tickets were not correct. Without waiting for the agent's next move, we quickly walked around the station instead of through it and started running through about a foot of snow. It was snowing heavily as we circled a hill or small mountain that kept us out of the view of the station agent. We ran across fields and over fences at a fast pace, expecting our tracks soon to be covered by the falling snow. We hoped the snow would be helpful if they tried to use dogs to find us. One of the more encouraging things about our movement was that we saw no houses or people. This looked like an area that could provide a safe place to hide.

The Guillon Family

Kenneth Shaver and I were the only Americans to stay at the Guillon home during the war. They were not part of the organized resistance, and their location next to the home where the German officers were housed meant great risk if they did anything unusual. Therefore, they, like most people trying to survive under occupation, followed a routine that did not draw attention to themselves. Their small acreage provided much of their food, but little was left over. In spite of that, when we suddenly appeared asking for help for one night, they responded to our needs.

After the Allied troops had advanced to their area, following the invasion, the Ninth Air Force took over the airfield the Germans had been using. The Americans used it as a fighter base. At that time, George Guillon was attracted to the base and did what he could to help, working there until the Americans left to return home. During that time, he was exposed to and learned the English language. A few years later, he was to serve time with the French army in Vietnam. From there he returned home to work for the French Government as an instrument technician. When we saw him in 1983 and 1985, he, his wife, and son were living at the home where we had stayed, and his job was nearby.

When George met us at the Brétigny railroad station in 1985, he drove us directly to his home. He was surprised that I identified the place as soon as it came into view and also pointed out the large house which the German officers had occupied. The picture of the Guillon home had remained in my mind. The house had been maintained as it was with the fence, gate and sidewalk unchanged. Surrounded by fruit trees and a large garden, the house and yard brought back memories of two young airmen in unknown territory seeking help from friendly people.

Mr. Gabriel Guillon was in failing health when Kenneth Shaver visited the family in 1972, and he died soon after that. He was always proud of the fact that he and his family had helped Ken and me. We are pleased that the Germans never knew they had helped us and that no harm had come to them.

Before my wife and I visited in 1983, Mrs. Guillon had retired, turned the home over to George, and had moved to St. Astier near Perigueux, France. That is where we visited her in 1985. She was 91 years old, very alert, living alone, and tending her own garden. She knew from talking on the phone with George that we were in France and intended to see her, but at no set time and date. Yet when with the help of some neighbors we located her, there was no question that we knew each other. We both shed a few tears of joy. She had saved two bottles of clear cherry wine which she had made in the summer of 1944. One of those she had given to Ken in 1972. The other she had saved for me. It reflected a strong belief in our eventual return. She had waited 41 years for me to return, and that required great faith. I am glad that we justified her faith and that the visit gave her some recognition at an age when people are often overlooked. Our visit with her was enriched by a young French girl who could speak English and who helped us exchange information.

While a student, George had developed a liking for Americans from what he learned. That feeling had been reinforced when he spent time with the men of the Ninth Air Force as they used the local airfield. To us he expressed great pleasure in having true American friends. I know that he and his parents earned that friendship at great personal risk, and I am thankful that Ken got back to thank them while Gabriel Guillon was still alive.

Clayton pauses at the yard gate with George Guillon, who was 17 years of age when the Guillons took him in 27 February 1944.

George and Clayton at the spot where they first met in front of the Guillon home in Brétigny-sur-Orge south of Paris, France.

Clayton presents a certificate of appreciation from the Air Force Escape and Evasion Society, and President Reagan, to Mme. Eva Guillon who is young at the age of 91.

Chapter 10

A Leap into the Unknown

Our jump from the train was a leap into the unknown. After walking several kilometers, we came to a small country road that showed little sign of being traveled. It appeared safe and offered better walking than in the fields. We liked the beauty and quiet of the country all covered with snow, and yet we felt very much alone as we chose a direction and began walking on the road.

We soon entered an area that was part of a farmstead, and we were greeted by the barking of dogs. After more than 20 hours of traveling alone on and off trains, we were tired and hungry. The barking dogs had announced our presence, so it was time to see if we could get either food or directions or both.

As we approached the house, we were impressed with its sturdiness and its very old appearance. There was much stone, and as we knocked on the door, we could see the walls were more than a foot thick. A lady answered our knock and stood erect as she watched and listened to us trying to identify ourselves and make a case for food and help. Then she invited us in and indicated we should sit down near the fireplace. It was the largest fireplace I had ever seen, and it provided heat as well as a place to do some cooking in iron kettles.

We had been invited in by the lady of the house, and we were soon joined by a couple of small children and two young men. Apparently, this was a family gathering that was trying to find a way to help us. We were fed, and as one of the young men left the gathering, we understood this family had no room for us, but they knew someone who might. At least they wanted us to be warm and comfortable in the safety of their home while they did some investigating for us. They assured us that we were still in France in a rural area that was not swarming with Germans.

The young man who had left the house earlier returned and looked as though he had had some success. In terms of time, it did not seem that he could have gone very far to make the contact. The family indicated we should wait for someone who would be coming for us.

The wait was not long, but it was late in the afternoon when a man a few years older than we appeared and invited us to follow him to his house. The walk would be only a few kilometers, but it seemed important that we complete the trip before dark. We had confidence in these people because they were sincere in their behavior and appeared willing to take risks to help us. The rural setting also served to remove our thoughts from some of the more hair-raising experiences we had been through earlier.

The snow was still falling when we arrived at our new location just before dark. The walk had gone without incident, and even though we had apparently been following roads, our tracks would soon be covered with snow. At our new location, a beautiful stone house with steps up to the door, we entered the yard through a metal gate with stone posts on either side. With the stone and metal fence along the road in front of the house it would be difficult for anyone to arrive undetected.

Inside we found a home that was warm and inviting. It belonged to our guide, Réne Beffera, and his lovely wife, Anne-Marie. No one could have given us a warmer welcome than they did. There were no children, but there was a family that lived in another house on the same farmstead. That family did much of the farming for the Befferas. Réne seemed to go and come when it was necessary, but he maintained a low profile. We learned that he had been called into the French army and taken prisoner by the Germans during the fighting. He had escaped from prison and returned home where French officials released him from his military obligation. France had surrendered, and formally they were not at war. While he had the necessary papers and every right to be at home, I am sure he did not want the German soldiers who might pass through the area to become aware that he was an escaped prisoner of war. Nevertheless, he and Anne-Marie accepted responsibility for us without hesitating. We were, and still are, very thankful they did.

I have wonderful memories of that home, beginning with those first moments when we were led into a large room used for dining and sitting. For me the focal point was a large stone fireplace along the outer wall. It was every bit as large as the one in the house we had just left, and there was a warm fire glowing in it. It was so large that they had built-in seats inside the chimney on both sides of the fire, and each seat was large enough to accommodate two people. Overhead in the chimney were hangers used for smoking meat. Swinging hangers and other facilities in addition made it possible to cook at the fireplace.

We quickly accepted their invitation to sit beside the fire where we could be warm and dry out our wet shoes. I could not believe that the fireplace and chimney could be so designed that we were able to sit in the chimney beside a warm fire without having it too hot for our faces. That fireplace provided an excellent center for many a warm and friendly conversation while we stayed with the Befferas.

With the very first meal, we learned that Anne-Marie was a fantastic cook as well as a warm and caring person. With their own farm produce, food never seemed to be in short supply. They also had a good source of wine and cheese. With plenty of milk and her culinary skills, Anne-Marie was even able to make ersatz coffee that tasted good. She brewed it from grain which had been parched until brown.

The excellent meal, sincere fellowship, and warm fire were a real blessing for a couple of scared Americans who had been standing on a train most of their 24 previous hours. We had seldom been in a real bed during the last weeks, and the stress of the total situation showed in our faces. The Befferas were determined to make things more pleasant for us, and they did.

With the calming effect that comes from a full stomach and the warmth of their hospitality, we were ready to retire for the night, but the Befferas wanted to do one more thing to make certain we would sleep well, so they provided us with a nightcap of warm wine. It was prepared on the stove from their table wine in a process I have never been able to duplicate. As Réne led us up the stairs to retire, Ken and I remarked that it would be a perfect night if we could have a bed as large as a double bed to sleep in. To our surprise, we were each given a double bed and separate rooms. To add to that luxury, we were also provided pajamas to sleep in. It was all more than we could have wished for, and we slept so soundly that it was mid-morning before we awoke.

Everyone had been thinking of our comfort and not about the danger of our presence. In retrospect, it was a special risk for the Befferas to have provided us with separate beds. It turned out all right, and we had separate rooms as long as we were there. But if the Germans had come while we were there and quickly searched the house it would have caused problems for all of us. The Befferas might have explained the use of two bedrooms, but it would have been difficult to explain why two people were using three bedrooms. I am very glad it worked out OK the way Réne and Anne-Marie arranged it. The beds were good. and the down-filled quilts were elegant and warm.

From our very first meeting and the first hours in their home, the Befferas made it clear they would help us in any way they could. If we wanted to go to Spain, they would help us. But while we were in their home, they would do everything possible to make us feel comfortable there. They also made it clear that they did not want us to make an unescorted exit from their place. It was evident to them we had demonstrated more luck than knowledge while traveling on our own in France.

We knew only a few words of French, and the Befferas knew only a few words of English. While there, we found that sign language, facial expressions, and the use of some props went a long way in helping us communicate with each other.

With a map, they showed us we were in central France between Mauriac and Aurillac. The train we had jumped off of was on its way to Aurillac, where there would have been a connection for Toulouse, but we were probably fortunate we had not stayed on the train and tried to make the transfer.

The second day we were at their home, Réne made a trip by train to Aurillac to see what he could do about getting some help for us. We also realized that Aurillac was probably the nearest location where some contact might be made to do something about verifying our identity. We knew that the Germans constantly tried to infiltrate any group that might help escaping fliers. It was thus important that we assist our helpers to establish our correct identities. To do this, we gave Réne a minimum, but necessary amount of critical information about ourselves when he told us he was going to Aurillac.

The distance was not great, but to make the trip by train, find the contacts he needed, and return meant a long day for Réne, so it was late when he returned from Aurillac and assured us there would be help. It would take some time, and we were to stay in his home where we could be safe and well cared for.

At the Befferas' our care was the best, and in the weeks that followed we gained weight from being fed so well. We were very comfortable, even though we were not content with how long we had to wait to be moved on toward Spain. A number of things occurred while we were with Réne and Anne-Marie which helped keep us from becoming bored. They had some visitors who were close friends and relatives who knew we were there.

One of the most regular visitors was an older man I thought at the time was Réne's father. He came by several times and on one occasion had a young black boy with him. I understood the lad's home was Marseilles. He was one of many children staying in central France where they thought fighting was less likely to occur.

One day, several people came to the house and were hosted in the parlor. Ken and I were invited to join them, and we were introduced to a drink called Calvados. It was clear and was served in tiny shot-like glasses. With it, people were also offered lumps of sugar. Although I had never drunk much, the amount we were served seemed insignificant, so I followed the lead of the few who did not take sugar. When we raised the glasses to our lips, I drank all of it. Then I realized the wise ones were those that had taken a lump of sugar. My drink burned all the way to my toes. While I tried to carry it off as if nothing was wrong, I understood the wisdom of dipping a lump of sugar into the drink and sucking it from the sugar. Mine had been an experience I would not repeat.

With the small group that had gathered was a young French lady who spoke some English. Even though time did not permit a lot of conversation with her, it was nice to talk with someone who did understand our language.

In our stay of three weeks with the Befferas, we were constantly amazed at the excellent meals which Anne-Marie prepared and served. She introduced us to a number of new and delicious dishes. One was a fresh egg on a piece of cured ham cooked in a frying pan on top of the stove. My wife and I have tried to duplicate the technique several times, but we have never succeeded.

Our differences in eating habits were noticeable at times, but the most memorable was the time Anne-Marie cooked and served freshly caught minnows. Réne had used a small minnow trap in a clear cold mountain stream to catch a couple of dozen plump shiny minnows, each about one and one half inches long. These were brought to the kitchen while very much alive and poured into a frying pan containing hot butter. It was no small trick to catch those that kept jumping out. But Anne-Marie succeeded, and they were fried to a crisp and served with a dash of malt vinegar. This was a special delicacy, and they expected Ken and me to eat most of them. While our behavior was dictated by the etiquette of guests, I have to admit that putting manners over matter was a struggle for us. We finally finished the minnows as expected, but it was not easy!

When we expressed our need for more exercise, we were taken outside one nice sunny day and across the road for a long walk through the fields. Another man, who may have been their farmer, accompanied the four of us, and we saw the small mountain stream from which the minnows had been taken. Réne enjoyed fishing, and while he expressed a desire to take us fishing, we knew that involved too much risk. We could more safely be taken for other short walks in the fields, always being careful not to go far, and trying to make certain we were not observed leaving or entering the Beffera home.

One day we were informed that a carpenter was coming to put a special wall in the basement which would create a room that had two purposes — one, to provide a place where arms could be hidden, the other, to make a place where Ken and I could hide if necessary. When it was finished, Réne took us down the basement steps and showed us how to press certain vertical boards that would open to create a passageway. Once we were on the other side, these boards could be closed and held shut to provide a solid wall. The false wall appeared as a protective cover for the foundation of the house, not as a wall for a room.

A newspaper would appear at the house once in a while, and we tried to read it. From the papers we could figure out some of the events being reported, especially if there were some pictures. One such picture really got our attention. It was an artist's conception of a B-17. The drawing was being used to explain the great odds the German pilots were faced with when they attacked formations of American bombers. The drawing made the B-17 look as though it had at least twice as much fire power as it actually had. In all fairness, there had been some experimenting with a few B-17's. They were equipped with additional fire power by eliminating most of the bomb load. One of these specially equipped planes in a formation of regular bombers might be used to sucker the Germans into encountering more than they expected. The artist and the writer had combined to make the special B-17 out to be the regular plane. Then to their concept they added plenty of exaggeration just for good measure. At this point in the war, the Allied forces had command of the air night and day. Germany was searching for stories that would help justify or explain what was happening. However, I believe most of the people, especially those in the resistance, saw the propaganda for what it was.

Ken and I had a feeling for what was and was not happening. Spring was approaching, and there was certain to be an invasion in the not too distant future. As much as we had appreciated our time with the Befferas, we felt our stay was becoming too long. Once, while discussing our concern with Réne, he expressed their expectation for an invasion in the near future. He also indicated that the resistance forces would need officers to help lead them once the invasion began. We got the message, whether our interpretation was right or wrong, that we were being detained to help lead the resistance forces. That was not an adventure we could look forward to, so we explained that we were trained for the air and not the ground and that it would be better for us to return to England and if necessary fight in the air. We also indicated we would again try traveling on our own to Spain if there was no help available.

Mr. Beffera made another trip to see what help he could get for us and returned with the message that we would be moved to another point in preparation for our trip to Spain. After three weeks with wonderful people who really made us feel at home, we would be leaving with mixed emotions. We were going to be on the move again, but there was no way we could expect to repeat the feeling of safety and the likeness of home that we had had with the Befferas.

I had some correspondence with the Befferas after the war, so I knew they had survived. My return visit to their home came in 1985 with many regrets that it had not been sooner because Réne died 24 March 1985 at the age of 73, before my wife and I arrived there in July.

Anne-Marie was again the gracious hostess and excellent cook. We sat inside the chimney of the fireplace and slept in the same bedroom I had been in 41 years before. Their home escaped damage from the war and reflected the good care and improvements it had received. There is a family that still tills and cares for the farm.

We learned that Anne-Marie had taught school and Réne had been a sergeant in the French army when he was taken prisoner by the Germans. It was in 1940 when he escaped and returned home. Anne-Marie and Réne were a part of the resistance almost from the beginning of the occupation. They were in the Resistance Organization of the Department of Cantal in France. It was affiliated with the FFI (Forces Francaises de l'Interieur). Since the routes used to move evading Allied airmen did not cross Cantal, Ken Shaver and I were the only Americans the Befferas took in and hid. However, they did aid the resisters and provided food and shelter on various occasions. One such incident came close to being fatal for Réne and perhaps Anne-Marie.

On 9 July 1944, which was some three months after Ken and I had left their home and one month after the invasion, Réne and Anne-Marie were housing two resistance leaders. One was Commandant Réne Gregoire, Chief of the Secret Army for the Cantal. Before the war he had been an engineer specialist in the building of dams to produce electricity and had lived at Aurillac. The other was Jean Lepine (code name Réne), Chief of the Civil Organization of Resistance in the Department of Cantal. Before the war he had been a car seller in Bordeaux. He came to Massie near Banille, where the Befferas lived, to participate in the resistance. These two men with top responsibilities had come to the Befferas' house after the disaster of Mont-Mouchet where many Maquisards were killed by the Germans.

On this eventful date, there was an evening meeting held at the Hotel Dexpert at Riomes Montagnes, a little town about 40 km northeast of Banille. The purpose of the meeting was to organize the Resistance of the Departmental Police. The main participants were: Oswald, Arthur Athene (code name Greco), Commandants Chastang, Monier, and Réne Gregoire. The Germans made an attack on the meeting and killed three men, Réne Gregoire, Monier, and Réne Laurent.

Réne Beffera had been scheduled to attend that meeting, but some emergency arose at the farm, and he was unable to go. Anne-Marie doesn't remember why Jean Lepine did not go, but other events of that evening are clear. A driver took Commandant Réne Gregoire to the meeting, and they were both going to return to spend the night at Befferas'. The hour came and went when they were expected back. Then, well past midnight, there was a knock at the door. It was the driver. He had parked the car and hidden nearby but had not gone into the meeting. He saw the shooting, learned that Réne Gregoire had been killed, left the car so as not to be followed, then walked and ran back to Befferas' to report the incident.

The farm emergency had kept Réne Beffera from the fatal meeting, and the driver's caution had kept the Germans from being led to the Befferas. Jean Lepine also survived the war and died at Aurillac well after 1944.

Mistakes Kenneth Shaver and I made in our travels caused the Befferas to help us two airmen, but their resistance efforts went much further. This brief story also helps to give some little example of how the Resistance was organized to deter or to sabotage the Germans' occupational efforts.

When I asked Anne-Marie why they chose to help Ken and me she said, "It was not a choice; we considered this helping as a natural part of our fight against the occupiers of our country." We're grateful for that attitude. And here I must also express my appreciation to Anne-Marie's cousin Jean Delery and his wife Marie-Catherine of Montlhery, France, for helping us research the story.

The Beffera home with their tennant house farther back from the road.

Réne Beffera with a great catch in September 1968. He loved to fish and was willing to risk everything to hide Clayton David and Kenneth Shaver for three weeks and make certain they were well cared for.

"Scotty" and Clayton David with Anne-Marie Beffera in front of her home in 1985.

Anne-Marie joins Clayton on one of the two seats inside the chimney of the fireplace in the Beffera home.

Chapter 11

The Free French Connection

Since our inability to speak French limited normal verbal communications, I do not believe the lump in my throat was too noticeable when we left the Beffera home, although I am sure we were all four holding back a few tears. A feeling of closeness develops when people share a common danger for some period of time, especially when they are aware constantly of the fine line between life and death even as they pray and hope for the best.

It was mid-afternoon when a car operating on coke gas appeared, and Ken and I were invited to take our first ride in what was called a "gazogene." As we bade farewell to the Befferas, our new guide drove off with us in the back seat. The road was level, and we were pleased with how well the gazogene was running. Apparently it had a fresh charge of coke which was being burned in a 55 gallon metal drum mounted on the rear bumper. Some kilometers later and on a very mountainous road, we became aware of the limitations of this source of energy. We had driven steadily but not fast. Now, while trying to go up a long and constant incline, the car stalled. We did not see any houses or people to be concerned about, but this was a new experience for us. The driver took it all in stride as he got out of the car and walked around to the rear. There he inserted a crowbar-like piece of metal into an opening in the steel drum and stirred the coke so that it would burn better. In a few minutes the coke was again releasing enough gas to power the car, and we drove on.

It was 30 kilometers or more from the Beffera house to our next stop, where we spent the night at the home of Henri Pontier. His son, Réne who spoke English, escorted us from the gazogene to the house. The area seemed more remote and less populated than any other place we had been. That was fine with us because we felt that fewer people meant less risk.

The next day, a young man, perhaps it was again Réne, took us into the mountains on foot. In this remote area there were only logging roads, and we saw men using oxen to do farming and logging. The oxen were slow but dependable. They could get along on hay and pasture with very little grain. While they did not require petrol like the tractors I was used to seeing on farms, they were even slower than the horses and mules we had used on the farm years before. After our experience with tractors and flying, this one was like stepping into a reverse time capsule.

There in the mountains, our hide-out was an old mill which was not being operated. There we joined about six young men who belonged to the Free French or Maquis. For the first time in all of our travels we saw our helpers bearing arms. These men appeared able to defend themselves in a limited skirmish or to conduct a small hit and run attack if advisable. Coming together with these people was an introduction to a different aspect of what takes place in occupied territory during a war. (A maquis is a scrubwooded upland, but it came to mean a new form of resistance: armed camps in the woods, ready for combat. As the Maquis grew, it needed arms, training, leadership, and food. Individuals of the Maquis are commonly referred to as Maquisards.)

The old mill had a fireplace in one end of the room on the first floor. The room contained a picnic-style table and some chairs. Several doors or openings could provide for a quick exit or entrance to the rooms and this feature made the mill a good hide-out. The mill was built into the side of the hill, and the mow on the second floor could be entered at ground level from the outside or by a ladder from the inside. We slept in the mow on some hay.

Some of the men seemed to go and come as if they were spending part of their time at work or in their homes nearby. Certain members of the group were present all of the time. It seemed they were from another place in France and here they could hide from the Germans and be active members of the French Resistance.

Ken and I were permitted to walk in the woods, but we did not stray very far from the old mill. We did not want to make the mistake of walking into a place of danger, and our group did not seem to want us to see everything in the area. One day while we were walking in the woods scouting around to see what the area was like, we had a real scare. It was very quiet in the woods, and we did not expect to have the silence broken. A sudden noise almost under our feet sent our hearts racing. Our momentary scare was over when we saw it was only a mountain grouse, but the noise it made leaving its nest — unbeliev-able. The reality of being behind enemy lines had a tendency to keep us on edge, even in a remote area where the only people we saw were friends.

On another occasion we walked into a heavy thicket and came upon a carefully hidden truck so well camouflaged that it could only be seen from a few feet away and certainly not from the air. When Ken made a comment about our find, one member of the group made it clear that they knew it was there. They had not intended to share that information with us and preferred that we not snoop too much.

There was plenty of food at the mill, but not much cooking was done. Each person shifted for himself, and people spent a lot of time sitting around the table talking. That was where the men also sat to clean and care for their guns. During one of those times, Ken and I were sitting with our backs to the fireplace talking to a young man who was cleaning his gun on the other side of the table. Suddenly a shot rang out and a bullet whizzed over our heads. The man had failed to make certain the gun was empty before starting to clean it and had accidently discharged a bullet left in the chamber. He got up as if unconcerned about the incident, discharged the empty shell casing from his gun, and walked around the table to the fireplace. He spotted the bullet which had just missed us lodged in the wooden mantel over the fireplace, took a pencil from his pocket and drew a circle around the bullet as if he had just hit the bulls-eye of a target, returned to his seat, and proceeded to finish cleaning his gun. He made no apology and no comment. It was as if nothing had happened, and it made us wonder how safe we really were. From then on, we were more aware at all times about what our friends were doing.

It was a loose-knit group that did not appear to be a well-trained and well-disciplined unit. We quickly learned that the group had a primary mission in the scheme of things, however. They were not far from a grass-covered mountain top which had been cleared of trees. The grassy area was still surrounded by trees, and the terrain made it possible to hide near the top of the mountain. They showed us this area and some covered dugouts around the clearing. All of this was set up as a drop zone for Allied fliers to use at night. There were several such places throughout France.

In preparing for us to participate in one of their missions, they took us through the complete process. They had a radio in the old mill, and it was always turned on at noon so they could listen to the British broadcasting station. At noon a coded message would indicate if a drop was planned for that night. At 6:00 pm they would listen again for a coded message to see whether or not the mission was still on. One day, the message at noon indicated a drop was planned for that night, and so during the afternoon, we went through a practice run in preparation for the mission. We went to the mountain top, and the men dispersed around it. Certain men would be using flashlights to pinpoint the drop area when they heard the plane arriving at the predetermined time. All supplies dropped would have to be removed from the clearing and hidden in the fewest minutes possible. If personnel were dropped, the same urgency existed. Timing was critical because German aircraft might be expected to try and follow the British or American plane. The Germans would try to shoot the airplane down or drop flares to see the drop area and the activity on the ground. A quick response on the ground was the best way to avoid having the drop zone spotted and to protect the items that were dropped.

After we went through our practice run on the mountain top, we returned to the old mill to await the 6:00 pm news, hopeful of a confirmation that the mission was still on. We were all disappointed when the coded confirmation was not given. The weather was good for making a drop, so the men in our group concluded that a drop to another location had been given priority. Only a limited number of missions of that kind could be flown because too many of them drew extra attention. Too many drops to one location could even create supply dispersal problems on the ground. While we were with the group, there was one more noon message that indicated a drop was planned, but it did not get evening confirmation. As a result, we never participated in receiving a drop, but the practice run did give us some feel for what went on and a better understanding of their objectives when we later became a part of their dispersal system.

Only a limited amount of English was spoken at that mountain hide-out, but the exchange of nonverbal expressions was sufficient to produce some understanding of the men and their thoughts. None of these young men had first-hand knowledge about the United States. However, the success the Americans had enjoyed at the 1936 Olympics in Berlin and the media's references to baseball and other sports in the United States caused them to respect Americans' athletic accomplishments.

Other ideas these men had about Americans came from cowboy and Indian movies and gangster movies. When someone mentioned Chicago, there was a pantomime alluding to guns and gangsters. They showed respect for Ken and me because we were fliers and we had participated in missions against a common enemy, Germany. In their dedication to the resistance movement, they experienced a kinship with us.

The last night we were to stay at this camp was a Saturday. That same night the Maquisards planned to conduct a special mission. They considered the Vichy police traitors to the resistance movement because they worked with the Germans and in many ways they were considered more dangerous than the Germans. They were usually local Frenchmen who knew the community, the people in it, and very often people's feelings about the German occupation. They also had a better chance than the Germans did at finding out about local activities. People were more apt to let their guard down or even trade information for a favor with the Vichy police than they were with the Germans.

By essentially working for the Germans, the Vichy policemen had access to many items that were in scarce supply. On this occasion, a local Vichy policeman had a daughter who was getting married. This small resistance group we were with had received information about the plans for the wedding and the reception. In comparison to the general standards at the time, this was going to be an elaborate wedding. It would be climaxed by a reception with plenty of food and wine, much of which had already been obtained and stored for the occasion. The timing had to be right, but the situation presented two opportunities. One was a chance for this group of the Free French to secure a supply of food and wine. The other was a chance to get something away from the Vichy policeman that would be difficult if not impossible to replace on short notice. Since the opportunities outweighed the risk involved, the group had made a decision to go for it.

The truck we had found in the thicket would be used to transport some of the personnel and to return the items to the camp. Ken and I were told about their plans and invited to join them. They were confident and sufficiently armed to win if using the weapons became necessary. In spite of their apparent ability to succeed against almost any odds, Ken and I turned down their invitation and stayed at camp. We figured our inability to communicate in French might endanger the success of their mission as well as ourselves.

Well after dark, the men took the truck and left the camp area. We remained alone and later went to the mow to sleep. We had no idea about how far they were going or how long it would take for them to complete the mission and return. We expected the men to be able to combine the element of surprise, their potential power of arms, and perhaps some inside information or help in a way that the mission could be achieved safely.

We were awakened a little before midnight and invited to the room below to join in celebrating their success. Naturally we responded, and even though we did not know how much loot they had expected to get, we concluded from their behavior and up-beat attitude that they had succeeded in getting as much or more than expected. The food consisted of several smoked hams, a supply of cheese, at least one barrel of table wine, several bottles of cognac, several cases of various wines and a few bushels of apples. The men indicated their biggest problem may have been getting everything on the truck and back to camp. We did not see everything they had captured because they left part of it on the truck and hidden in the thicket. From their comments, we got the feeling that their greatest reward had come from watching the behavior of the Vichy policeman, who had had to watch helplessly as they carried off the food and wine he had been collecting and hoarding for weeks. Some might call it sweet revenge against a regime of collaborators and traitors.

From that incident I did learn at least two things. One was that an individual like the Vichy policeman, who is a traitor to his country-men for short-term personal or political gain, may find there is a price to pay. That incident may have been one of the less severe penalties. The other lesson was more personal. To appreciate the value of the Maquisards' bounty, we were expected to sample the various wines and cognac they had secured. We tried to respond to their wishes and not insult our hosts. In our efforts to show appreciation for their achievements and their hospitality, we learned the price one pays for mixing drinks or for over-indulgence. The results affected me for more than 24 hours, and it was an experience I have never repeated.

Since we never knew the names of the young men in this small group of resistance fighters or where their homes were, I have no way of knowing about actual skirmishes they became involved in or how many of them survived the war. But there are many monuments erected throughout France in memory of the Maquisards, their resistance activities, and the lives that were lost.

Soon after the war I heard from Réne Pontier. He is the son of the late Henri Pontier with whom we stayed before going to the Maquis' hiding place. He was the one who escorted us to his father's home. We have maintained some contact over the years, and from him we have learned much.

Réne Pontier was involved in security work with the Maquis and first worked from Aurillac, France. He was contacted about us by Bernard Cournil, who had been contacted by the Chief of the local resistance, Henri Tricot. Réne was contacted because he spoke English. Then as he remembers, "Our radio specialist announced to the Allied Services in Great Britain your names and gave many precise informations about your 'Odyssey,' your next evasion, and arrival in Great Britain."

After that, Réne left the area and moved several times to avoid being captured by the Gestapo, which hunted him and his associates constantly. He reports:

> In Montauban, near Toulouse, a friend who was in my room jumped from the window of the second floor and was killed on a bridge in Montauban while I fled by the door. I almost suffered the same adventure before being sent to the department of Hautes Pyrenees near the border of Spain. I stayed there to manage droppings and to search for new drop zones. Information was gathered and noted to determine which drop zones were or were not agreeable to the Services in Great Britain.

Réne's responsibilities with the drop zones also involved arranging security and accounting for the arms and other items they received by parachute from the Allied Forces in Great Britain. After the hostilities ceased, his work included collecting and accounting for the arms.

At the beginning of the war in 1940, Réne was a student and too young to be mobilized. After the war, he continued his education and became a teacher. When my wife and I had a delightful visit with him and his wife in 1985, he had retired. They were living at St. Cyr-sur-

Mer on the Mediterranean Sea east of Marseilles, and their son lived about an hour's drive away. Réne's father had died, and their house near Le Rouget was standing but unoccupied.

Although the Department of Cantal, where Ken and I lived with the Befferas and the Maquis, was not on an organized escape route for airmen, it was an important area for the Masquisards. Newspaper clippings supplied to me by Réne have shown the importance of the people who helped us and of the drop zone, "Chenier Field." Our Maquis helpers had responsibility for the security and the operation of Chenier Field. That our presence in the area required careful attention and special handling is not surprising.

France's battle against the invading Germans took place in the spring of 1940 and ended in defeat for France. Initially, the amount of occupational control by the German troops varied with the districts in France, the location, and the population density. Some of the areas with rough terrain, a small population, and limited transportation arteries received less attention from the Germans. The availability of places to hide made these areas advantageous for organizing, training, and equipping Masquisards to carry out sabotage and hit-and-run attacks against the Germans. One disadvantage was that, because the resistance groups did form and act in the rural areas, some of the most devastating acts of retalitation were carried out by the Germans against local people.

By November 1942, with the Germans occupying the Department of Cantal, the resistance was established at Aprajon-sur-Cere. It was organized under the movement of the Liberation of Sud (south); Armand Steel from Aurillac maintained the contacts. In time, Liberation Sud united with the other movements of the Resistance.

At the beginning of 1943, Bernard Cournil, who owned a garage at Rouget, rented a building in La Fontbelle in which to hide his men. In March 1943 the first Maquis, made up of approximately 25 men, organized by Bernard Cournil and Marcel Gaillard (alias "Gilardon") settled in La Fontbelle. La Verrerie is the name of the spot in Luzette at the bottom of the gorges of Cayla. When the group's hiding place was attacked on 19 June 1943 by units of the Germans' Automobile Guards from Cahors, the men had left the day before. Such was the advantage of small groups that could move quickly, hide, and act when needed.

In August of 1943, Bernard Cournil was contacted by Harold

Rovella of the S.A.P. (resistance section about landing and parachuting), to help establish a new field that could be used for drops and possibly airplanes. For five months Cournil and Rovella worked together to prepare the site called Chenier Field.

Chenier Field was under the Toulouse S.A.P. whose leaders, in their order of succession, were as follows: Rateau ("Pape"), Picard ("Sultan"), and Guillermin ("Pacha"). Their delegates of the department present at Chenier Field during February of 1944 were Rovella, Réne Pontier ("Sultan VII") and Jean Cotter. (Members of a group were identified by the leader who had enlisted them. Hence Réne Pontier ("Sultan VII") had been recruited by Picard whose code name was "Sultan." Each leader's name was that of a noble rank.)

In addition to his other duties, Bernard Cournil was the person responsible for Chenier Field along with agents one and two of the network which had a crew that kept growing until it included 16 men in 1944.

Chenier Field, selected because of its location, developed into one of the most important drop zones in the district. It was classified as "home depot." It included a radio-telephone for communications and a beacon called "Eureka," which was capable of signaling planes for a distance of 250 kilometers. In addition to receiving scheduled drops, it was used to receive the drops from planes which could not locate or drop at their primary drop zones. As a result, the men at Chenier Field had to stand watch from 7:00 pm until 4:00 am when drop missions were being flown into the area.

The field received its first parachutes at the end of August 1943. Rovella recorded about 137 parachutes for the month of January 1944. Parachutes lowered personnel as well as supplies to the ground. Since the field was the distribution center for three Resistance regions, R.N.6 (Auvergne), the R.4 (Toulouse, the law department) and the R.5 (Limousin), and was also the site of unscheduled drops, the number of parachutes it received during those critical months is not known exactly. An estimate puts the material received at Chenier Field at a minimum of 700 containers. The containers were loaded on carts belonging to Menevioles and the Fontabelle farms. From there, distribution was according to the destination.

In addition to the supplies which were dropped at Chenier, around 42 Allied agents parachuted onto the field to carry out various assignments. The number of agents landing there was greatest around the time of the Allied invasion on 6 June 1944.

Bernard Cournil played a role in helping Ken and me evade capture. He may have driven the gazogene in which we rode when we left the Befferas. He received from the British people "The King's Medal of Courage" in the cause of freedom. He was one of the very few Frenchmen to receive it. Bernard Cournil died in 1982.

It is interesting to look back and realize how important our friends, Cournil's Maquis, in that quiet, remote, and beautiful part of France were to the Resistance movement. Like the men who landed at Omaha Beach, many of them and their friends died for the cause of freedom.

Réne Pontier ("Sultan VII") accepts his certificate of appreciation at his home in St. Cyr-sur-Mer on the Mediterranean Sea east of Marseilles. Réne had helped with the security clearance on Clayton and Ken before taking them to his father's home and the Maquis camp.

"Claire" and Jean ("Sultan II") Arhex meet Clayton in Paris in 1985. It was the first time they had seen Clayton since escorting him in 1944. They had met Clayton and Ken at the Maquis camp and escorted them to the mountain guide outside of Pau, France, for their climb across the Pyrenees mountains.

"Claire," Jean, "Scotty," and Clayton met for dinner before the Davids left Paris for home in 1985.

Chapter 12

An Escort with a Lookout

The morning after we had joined our hosts in celebrating their successful raid, things were off to a slow start. It was almost noon, and a few of the men were not yet up and around when a lady and a man we had not seen before appeared on the scene. They were about my age, and the lady spoke English. They were both well composed and business-like in their approach to us. The lady, called "Claire," was about five feet three inches tall, slender, and attractive. The man, "André," was a full six feet tall and well built. They made a nice-looking couple, and they were better dressed than average. "Claire" would be our escort to the Pyrenees mountains which form the border between France and Spain. "André" would be nearby and serving as lookout to help assure our safety.

We learned from "Claire" that we would be going to a railroad station to catch a train to Toulouse. That was the destination we had been unable to reach on our own a month before. We also learned that most travelers carried suitcases, and that we would do likewise. It was about 1:00 pm when we said our goodbyes and left camp on foot for the station. "Claire" as our guide and "André" as the lookout worked so well together that to us "André" went almost unnoticed.

We reached the station in mid-afternoon and entered a cafe nearby to have some food and wait for the train. I had succeeded in eating an apple earlier, and here I decided some soup might be the easiest thing for my stomach. It was, and I ate it without any problem. While at the cafe, we received the suitcases we were to carry. I believe the maneuver which had made the arrival of the suitcases possible had been directed by "André."

This was our first exposure to how the distribution system from the aerial drop zone worked. The suitcases were small and rather heavy. We were to carry one in each hand, but not to open them. We were told that among other items, the suitcases would contain machine guns, ammunition, and hand grenades. These would be distributed later to the French for use once the invasion began.

"Claire" wanted us to know how successful their organization had been in receiving and distributing the arms dropped to them. She indicated they were sufficiently organized and supplied with arms so that the French Resistance would be able to take over and control most of the area and many of the towns in Southern France. That would happen when the invasion began and they were told it was time to take action. History shows they were basically correct in their assessment. There were times when they may have tried to do too much and the Germans took offensive action that cost many French people their lives. Nevertheless, their achievements were many, and what may have been one of the most important occurred soon after the invasion.

One of Rommel's elite combat units, the Reich Armored Division, was in the south of the district of Dordogne near Cantal. On 7 June, the second day of the invasion, Rommel called for that unit to move quickly to be used against the Allied beachheads in Normandy. It was a critical moment in the battle, and had the unit arrived in the following days, it might well have turned the battle against the Allies. The division had tremendous fire power and crack fighting units.

Resistance forces in the Dordogne were ordered into action against that armored division. They attacked with bazookas, machine guns, and hand grenades. Along the direct route the division was traveling, they blew up bridges and railroads, which forced the Germans to take alternate routes. While the Resistance fighters were sacrificing their lives to delay the Reich, they also relayed intelligence information to London. London relayed the data to the RAF, and soon fighters and bombers of the Allied forces were shooting up the columns of the crack armored division.

The division was both delayed and weakened by the combined efforts of the Allied Air Forces and the Resistance. Only a few tanks managed to get through to Normandy a week or more later, too late to have any big influence on the battle. As a result of what happened to the Reich Division, the German High Command instructed other divisions heading north from the area of Montabaun and Toulouse to circle around Dordogne. Two powerful forces, the Gross-Deutschland and the Goering Divisions, detoured to avoid the French Resistance forces. They ran into them anyway, for the Resistance was active everywhere. They also arrived too late for the battle of the beaches in Normandy.

It had been clear to us, there in the mountains before the invasion, that guiding Allied airmen out of France and across the Pyrenees was not the main mission to which these people were assigned. No doubt our delay at the Befferas and in the camp had been a matter of priorities. But we were grateful for their help, and they were doing a good job in taking care of us. We were glad we had convinced them to move us on, instead of staying to join them in the battles which were to come.

Our trip had been planned correctly, and the train ride to Toulouse went without incident. "Claire" told us that guards were not normally checking at the Toulouse railroad station on Sunday. For that reason, they had selected Sunday for our trip. She told us to walk some distance behind her when we got off the train to leave the station with our suitcases. If she or "André" detected danger, they would warn us. At that point, we would take total responsibility for our own actions. As we walked through the train station and out into the darkened city, I realized it was probably divine guidance and good luck, not bad luck as we had thought at the time, which had kept us from getting to Toulouse on our own. If we had arrived in Toulouse on our own, it would have been early on a Tuesday morning, not on a Sunday. With German guards or the Vichy police there to check us, there was a very good chance we would have been detected and arrested. Years later I learned that many of the Allied airmen who got as far as the area of Toulouse had indeed been arrested and taken to prison or worse. In fact, only about one half of the airmen who reached the Pyrenees mountains succeeded in reaching Spain. The others met fate in a variety of ways. Some were captured and became prisoners of war. A number were killed in shoot-outs with the Germans who attempted to capture them and their guides. Some died in falls or drowned while attempting to cross mountain streams. Then there were those who found it physically impossible to make the difficult trek and gave up. When they returned to the foot of the mountains, they were often spotted and captured.

We followed "Claire" as directed and walked a few blocks to an apartment in the residential area of the city where we were the overnight guests of an older lady. At the apartment, someone else took charge of our suitcases, and our role in making the delivery was complete. We took some satisfaction in returning a favor to the group that had helped us, but often wondered what price we would have paid if caught with the suitcases and their contents. We were glad to be rid of them, and I am confident the contents were put to good use.

Chapter 13

The Pyrenees —
Beauty and Mystery

"Claire" returned early the next morning to take us by train to Pau. Our helpers in Holland, Belgium, and Paris had told us they usually took the fliers from Toulouse south into the mountains toward the little country of Andorra, then guided them to the border and into Spain. Therefore, our train ride with "Claire" along the foothills of the Pyrenees from Toulouse via Tarbes to Pau was a much different route than we had expected. Later, we would understand why.

The date was 10 April, a beautiful spring day. As the train made its way along the side of the mountain range, we could see the beauty of the countryside. My farm experiences reminded me then of all the work that farmers had to do to get their crops started at that season of the year. The fields, vineyards, and orchards blended into the mountains capped with snow that glistened in the sunshine.

Near Lourdes or Tarbes, we saw a large white cross on the side of the mountain, and I thought it stood out like a good omen. The beauty of that train ride was such that I wished I could put the danger of the moment out of my mind and enjoy it like a person on vacation. But beneath all of that beauty was the mystery of what lay ahead for us. Who might lead us where? How many of us would there be? And how many teams of German guards would be trying to prevent us from crossing into Spain? Those questions and many more kept chasing through my mind and kept me from enjoying one of the most beautiful train rides I had ever had. It seemed very fitting that we were expecting soon to make our break from enemy-occupied land in spring, a time of hope and new life.

As the train pulled into Pau, I was quick to observe a large number of German soldiers. Looking more closely, I saw that they were not like the sharp looking young men we had seen in Paris and Brussels. Most of them looked older, and many had obviously been injured in battle. These were not the men you would expect to see preparing to defend against an invasion. They appeared physically incapable of putting down a large uprising from the Resistance or to launch a significant attack. When I asked "Claire" why they were at Pau in such large numbers, I learned that these Germans, casualties of the war, were using the hospitals and other facilities in the area for medical treatment and R & R (rest and recovery).

As I observed those German soldiers, my thoughts turned to the comments about how the French Resistance forces would take control of the small southern towns like Pau when the invasion was launched. Having seen some of the German soldiers in the area and having been exposed to some of the Free French personnel, I was willing to place my bets on the side of the French Resistance.

We had not seen "André" at all on this trip, but when we got off the train in Pau, people were waiting for us. I believe he had been busy somewhere making sure every thing went smoothly. We were driven by car several kilometers into a rural area at the foot of the mountains, let out alongside the road, and directed down a country lane to the barn in a farmstead. There, near Navarrenx, France, we would rest and prepare for our travels, which would begin on foot after dark.

"Claire" and "André" slipped from our view, and it would be many years before I would learn more about them, why they had been there when we needed them, and how the war had affected their lives. Each person involved in the resistance, regardless of the country, had his or her own story, but all had certain things in common. Some incident or personal feeling caused each to join in the resistance, and when the war was over, the survivors still had to try putting normal lives back together again.

When I learned more about "Claire" and "André," I was fascinated. Paule Viatel (Resistance code name "Claire") was a student of the German language. For many years she visited Germany, and during the entire school year of 1936-37 she studied at Fribourg-en-Brisgau, so she saw the rise of Nazism.

In June 1940, Paule was a young teacher of German in a secondary school. When France surrendered to Germany, she knew at once that she must struggle against the German occupation. She felt that it would be the downfall of civilization if Hitler was victorious. Her teaching job was terminated, and she was frustrated about how or with whom to resist.

Her opportunity came when a German professor at the College of Lyon, France, who knew her well asked her to work for the French intelligence services of Vichy, a second level position — not quite the Resistance, but almost. Her job was simply to read German newspapers and magazines, then translate into French the funeral notices and articles pertaining to the sciences such as raising crops and manufacturing synthetic petroleum. This unusual and monotonous work lasted for two years until November 1942 when the Germans moved into what had been known as the "free zone." Her job was eliminated, but as one activity closed, a new one opened up.

Newspaper men of the liberation interested Paule in the gathering of information, namely information about the movement of German troops. This really was a Resistance matter, and as "Claire" took on the more dangerous task, she was also asked to hide secret agents, some from London, in her apartment.

On 21 June 1943, a meeting was scheduled at Calurie, the suburb in the hills above Lyon. Expected there to develop and coordinate some critical plan were the heads of the Resistance. In spite of the secret methods used to arrange the meeting and to get the men to the designated place at a specific time some mistakes were made. With the meeting delayed for 45 minutes, the Gestapo Chief, Klaus Barbie, and his troops arrived just as the meeting was about to begin. There must have been a leak somewhere. It was quite a haul for Barbie. Among those arrested was Jean Moulin ("Max"), personal envoy of General de Gaulle, Chief of the Resistance. Jean Moulin died under torture without talking when interrogated.

The arrests at that meeting dealt a severe blow to the Resistance in general and came personally close to "Claire." One of the men arrested, and who died later in Germany, was Bruno Larat (Code name "Xavier"), a representative of the S.A.P. network for the area around Lyon, the R 1. Larat had been using "Claire's" apartment as his hide-out in Lyon. While she had faith that "Xavier" would die without telling anything, "Claire" could not take the risk. She ran toward Spain with no intention of withdrawing from the Resistance. She was welcomed in Toulouse and entrusted with a difficult mission, establishing an escape route toward Spain. The route must have its escorts, its relays, and its parachuting spots. She must not only organize the route but personally escort a group of evadees. That was among the most dangerous of all underground responsibilities.

The contacts in such a network were destroyed on a regular basis and the agents arrested. When one link was broken, a whole new chain had to be established. "Claire" was on one of her successful missions, between Chenier Field and the Spanish border, when she and "André" escorted Ken and me in mid-April 1944. But not all of her missions went as well as ours.

About a month later, in May 1944, "Claire" was leading a group of eight people toward Spain. In Toulouse, they got on the seven o'clock train for Saint-Gaudens and got off at Boussens, where they took a bus for Saint Girous. "Claire" got off at Laoave followed by the men she was leading and took a country road to Urau, where her relay, the village blacksmith, was waiting. The weather was good, the trip had been uneventful, and everything seemed easy. A frontwheel drive vehicle which "Claire" was accustomed to seeing approached them. Suddenly, the vehicle spun around in a cloud of dust, forcing her and her men into the ditch. Four men sprang from the vehicle with machine guns and revolvers drawn. "Claire" recognized the fifth man who was now standing behind the other four looking like a beaten dog. It was Maraval, the one who had helped her establish the network.

They were all ordered out of the ditch, and "Claire" was separated from the others. She was searched, interrogated, threatened and beaten. They knew she was the leader, but they beat everyone in the group with gun stocks as they were taken to a nearby farmyard. Then they, including Maraval, were locked in a room, and "Claire" came face to face with Maraval. She asked, "What are you doing, Maraval? Why are you with the Germans?"

He replied, "I was arrested in Toulouse. They took me into some woods and beat me. I did talk. I did talk."

"You are fortunate; there are no signs of the bruises you received," "Claire" commented, and Maraval dropped his head, ashamed.

The Germans returned and ordered the people out of the room, and while holding machine guns to their backs, had them stand with their faces to a wall. They ordered Maraval to join them and stated, "We are going to knock down-kill the blacksmith."

When they returned, they laughed and slapped Maraval on the back. The blacksmith had been shot!

"Claire," who was wounded and bleeding, was standing with the other prisoners. The Germans were talking, but they did not know that

"Claire" understood what they were saying. She detected a let-down in their surveillance as they ordered the farm wife to make them some pancakes. At that point, "Claire" asked for some fresh water so she could wash herself. The request was granted. In the house, she spotted an open window in a room with a partly open door. She entered the room and closed the door so that the policeman could not see her, then immediately jumped through the window and landed on the ground in back of the house. It was a sloping pasture field, and she found herself among a group of dumbfounded reapers. She ran as fast as she could across the open pasture and plunged into some undergrowth in the middle of briars.

She expected to hear shots, but there were none. Perhaps the Germans had been unable to fire. She ran through the country, through woods, yards and paths. Worn out, she kept going down hills and up slopes. Anything to put distance between her and the farm where her companions were being held. It was the only way to come out alive.

Suddenly, a man appeared at the turn of the road. It was Maraval, waiting there in the dusk. Thinking he must surely be waiting for her, "Claire" wondered if this might be the end. No! She took off again, changed direction, zig- zagging and escaped into the night. Apparently Maraval did not follow her. She went to the village Salies-du-Salat.

Dogs barked as she knocked on a door. A voice inside asked, "Who is there?" "Someone in trouble," was "Claire's" reply, and the voice came back, "Go away!" She kept going; she was barefoot with her shoes in her hand. At a turn in the road someone called out, "Who is there?" Weapons rattled! She threw herself into the ditch, and two car headlights came on. The car came closer and passed on. "Claire," squatting in the ditch, had not been seen. Saved one more time! She kept going, left the road and crossed fields for more saftey. When morning came, she stood exhausted in a hollow on the edge of the river. She looked down at the one shoe she was wearing and realized she must rest through the day to regain some strength for the following night.

At nightfall she started to walk again, but she was soon exhausted and famished. She felt empty-headed and discouraged, but her extraordinary will to live drove her on. When she stopped to collect her thoughts, she realized that she must have help. She needed to make contact with someone in the Resistance, but how was the challenge.

It was 6 am when she knocked on a door. It opened, and the woman standing before her looked at a bloody and beaten "Claire" with clothing torn by the efforts of her escape. When "Claire" asked for help, the woman told her to leave. Then an older lady called from inside to ask who was being told to leave and then said, "I've never turned a person in need away from my door. Let her come in." "Claire" entered and told her story. She showed them her sores and wounds, and they believed her. "We are going to help you," came their reply.

With their help, "Claire" was able to travel again and get to Boussens where she knew the cook at the Hotel de la Gare, who was a member of the network. The contact was made, the network was notified, and members took her that same night to a safe hiding place. The network then notified Toulouse, and a car was sent for "Claire." She was back in the fold to recuperate for awhile before resuming activities. The memories of the entire experience are still so strong that "Claire" cannot eat pancakes because it reminds her of those Germans who asked the farm lady to make pancakes for them.

After the invasion of 6 June 1944, "Claire" was helping Brigitte, their radio operator, decode messages. In July, one of the messages from London when decoded said, "If 'Claire' has escaped she must take the plane for London." What a shock: the plane would be landing that very night, and the secret field, Aire-sur-Adour, was some 60 kilometers away. She did not wait, said "Good-bye," and began her bicycle ride to the landing spot. On the road she was stopped, not by the Germans, but by the Maquis who took her to their place for interrogation. They did not believe her story, and just when she was sure the delay would keep her from meeting the plane, a man who knew her walked in and asked why she was there.

She was given assistance and rushed to the landing spot. There were only a few moments. A Hudson bomber plane from London landed momentarily, and she ran to it, climbed in, and they were off. When she looked about in the plane she saw "André," the man who had provided the lookout when she had escorted Ken and me nearly three months before. He had reached the plane and boarded before her. It had been some time since they had seen each other, and neither knew for certain what had happened to the other one.

Upon their arrival in England, "Claire" was assigned to the B.B.C. and used her langage skills to give messages and talk to the French people. Friends heard her in France and told her parents. That is how they found out she was still alive.

After the war was over, she returned to France to teach and to translate books from German into French.

When the Germans invaded France, Jean-Baptiste-Arhex was working in an airplane factory at Toulouse. He was Basque and had lived a free life in a small village between Pau and the French-Spanish border in le Pays Basque.

From the beginning, Jean knew that to resist the Germans he would have to give up his job and take on a new name, as the Gestapo and French police had him identified by his family name. Jean became known as "Andre," "Jainy Lafont" or "Sultan II." He was also recruited by Picard ("Sultan"), the same man who recruited Réne Pontier. "André" served with the Liberation Sud, The Armee Secret (AS) and Rejeaux Action R4 (S.A.P.), the parachute jumping and air supply unit of the Resistance.

I know now that it was no accident that Ken and I went from Pau and crossed the mountains through Basque country with a Basque guide. About those activities "André" said, "It was a part of my struggle. We had to search for arms, to transport them, to organize Maquis and the parachuting of arms coming from England." He was most active in the area from Toulouse south to the Spanish border, but what happened there was also related at times to activities north of Toulouse, where he and "Claire" met us at Chenier Field.

When "André" flew out of France in July 1944 with "Claire" to England, it was to prepare for training with a unit that would parachute back in at a later date and further north.

Nearly 40 years later when my wife and I were able to make contact with "André" and "Claire," we found it was Jean and Paule Andréx. They live in an apartment in Paris with a get-away villa some 90 kilometers northwest of Paris near Evreux. The villa's setting is tranquil and beautiful. I am sure it helps Jean to remember his childhood days in the scenic Basque country at the foot of the Pyrenees.

Jean married someone else soon after the war, and it was years later when Jean and Paule, who had worked together in the Resistance, came together again and were married. I have only known them as a team. Jean retired from his job as an atomic engineer in 1985, but Paule still translates German books into French for a publisher.

When I asked them about the effect their work in the resistance had on their personal lives, they both mentioned the difficulty in having to give up their real names for code names. After the war, the difficulty was building new lives with their real names and adjusting to all the change so they could again live normally. It would appear that they were successful on all counts, except I still call Paule "Claire." Each of them helped about 100 people, mostly French, evade the Germans and reach Spain. They often helped the same people, but it was all done at great personal risk as part of their resistance effort. I hope they enjoy many more peaceful years together. They have earned them.

Chapter 14

The Crossing

We were to meet our guide at the farm. Others who might be crossing the mountains with us would join us there. We were assured that our mountain guide knew the area very well. Perhaps he had crossed the same terrain many times while smuggling items across the French-Spanish border. We also had the feeling he would be — or had already been — paid for this trip.

This was rough but beautiful Basque country, and our guide was Basque. Living and walking in, around, and over the mountains was routine for this man, who was to be our guide until we reached Spain. It was emphasized that the trip would be difficult and very long, that we would travel much at night, and that the weather would not be good. We could expect rain, fog and clouds, which would make the trip more difficult, but on the other hand the bad weather would reduce our chances of being seen or caught by the German border guards. The Germans sent their patrols into these mountains on a regular basis especially to catch groups like ours.

A third person had joined Ken and me in Pau, and we were brought to the farm together. He was a French courier, and his job was to parachute into France with money, instructions, and other necessary items for the French Resistance. After making his delivery, he would walk across the mountains into Spain and eventually return to England. From there he would begin a similar assignment. He told us this would be the third time he had crossed these mountains. Providing safe passage for this man and others with similar duties was part of the mission assigned to the Resistance group we had become associated with. Helping downed fliers escape was not their primary mission and therefore, I have since learned, Ken and I were about the only fliers to receive assistance from this particular group. I am pleased that we successfully helped them in one of their primary missions when we delivered the arms and ammunition to Toulouse.

After dark, when it was time for us to start walking, another man, a

Spaniard who had apparently made his own arrangements with our Basque guide, joined our group. He said he had left Spain during the Spanish Revolution to avoid fighting in it and was trying to get back to his home.

Our group of four was an unusual combination with one objective keeping us together, to get safely across the mountains into Spain. The first night we walked on paths, lanes, and fields that would permit us to cover the greatest distance undetected. About daybreak, our guide told us to stop and wait in a safe spot while he walked ahead to check the barn and farm where we would rest and eat food. When he determined it was all clear, he returned for us and led us to the barn.

Our every move seemed to be on a schedule. When fog and clouds blanketed the area, we started moving again. That was about mid-afternoon. I remember thinking this was the first time this flatlander from Kansas had ever walked in the clouds. Darkness came early, and a light rain was falling on us. We continued to walk into what was perhaps the blackest night of my life.

The mountains were getting steeper, and we found we had to walk back and forth to create a more gradual incline rather than make a direct ascent, which would have been faster but more fatiguing. In doing this, we used paths the cows had made while grazing. When the night was at its darkest, we passed through some of the roughest terrain of all. When the walking was the most difficult and it was so dark we could not see three feet in front of our eyes, the guide had us walk with each man holding on to the coat tail of the man ahead of him. The man holding onto the guide had to make certain he did not lose his grip, or we might all be lost.

In this fashion, we proceeded in a steep climb beside a mountain stream. We could not see the stream, but we could hear the water below us. When we stopped to catch our breath, we would remain standing and continue to hang on to the coat tail of the man in front of us. No one wanted to risk having the group quietly move away without him.

Finally, we came to a point where the guide gathered us around him to say that we would be crossing a swinging foot bridge. We were to hang on to the sides with our hands while moving steadily ahead and across the bridge and not look down because it was inky black, and one misstep could cause one to fall several hundred feet to his death.

As I started across the bridge, that swaying, which goes with a swinging bridge when it's being walked on, had me wishing for a bridge which was rigid. I could hear the loud sound of rushing water hundreds of feet below, and I wondered about the sights we were missing this coal-black night. At the same time, I realized we were so high that anyone who crossed that bridge in daylight would be visible for quite some distance. I thanked God when we were all safely on the other side. The long climb up the mountain in the blackness of night, with rocks cutting at our shoes, climaxed with the swinging bridge, is unforgettable. I have often wondered if it would have been more frightening for us had we been able to see where we were going. It was a "Trust Walk" unlike any other I have ever experienced.

We were now high on the mountain within a few kilometers of the border. It was time to go into hiding before daybreak. The area was isolated, but if the weather cleared, we were high enough to be seen for some distance, especially if guards were watching the area through binoculars as they normally did. At the same time we were also ready to get off our feet and rest, which meant the guide had correctly estimated time, distance, and the limit of our endurance.

That afternoon, while the clouds continued to shroud the mountains, our guide started us moving again, back and forth up the mountain, up through the clouds. The snow covering the upper part of the mountain range slowed our progress, and by the time we reached an altitude above the clouds, darkness had come to the mountains. But this was not the all-restricting darkness of the previous night. We were above the clouds, and in the moonlight from a clear sky we could see how vast the area of snow there above the timberline was. We could see that the top of the mountain ridge was still some distance off. Meanwhile, the knee-deep snow and the high altitude were taking a toll on our energy.

The guide stopped to let us rest, and we reclined with our backs in the snow to make the best of our stop. It was quite cold, so the rest had to be a short one. At this point, the Spaniard indicated he could not go on. But we were not going to be denied the crossing after getting this close to the border. We felt it was important for all of us to top the mountain together. I remembered having saved the two Benzedrine pills from my escape kit for just such an emergency. Getting them out of my pocket, I gave one to the Spaniard. Then Ken and I shared the other one. We put some snow in our mouths and let it melt to help us swallow the pills. With some tugging and encouragement, we soon had the Spaniard on his feet and moving again. We pressed on!

Finally, in snow about waist-deep on ground that was probably high pasture land in the summer, we reached the crest of the mountain. The guide stopped and pointed out the border. France and Spain came together at the peak of the ridge which ran along the top of the mountain. That is where we were standing, and a down-hill trek would take us into Spain. The guide also pointed out a sheep herder's shed some distance below us which was used only during the summer months and would make a good place to rest. This was as far as the guide would take us. His obligation completed, he wanted to get off the highest part of the mountain back into France before daylight.

We four, who had the common objective of reaching Spain, could now slide in on our own. We started for the shepherd's cabin, but when we reached it, our objectives diverged. Ken and I decided to keep going to get further from the border before we might be seen and perhaps arrested. The Spaniard and the French courier stopped. The Spaniard hoped to get home without being detected. The French courier probably knew a route or had connections that would speed him on his way to England. Ken and I said farewell to these men with whom we had shared three nights and days. We never saw them or the guide again.

In our crossing we were fortunate to have encountered no Germans. Our guide clearly knew his business. We also were lucky to have had the stamina to make the climb with enough strength left over to help the Spaniard. That we were a small group worked to our advantage as did the rain, clouds, and darkness which were so disagreeable.

At that point we did not realize how fortunate we had been. We only knew that we had crossed into Spain. For me it was the climax of spending more than three months in enemy-occupied territory. For Ken it had been nearly five months. We were not certain about the future, but our adrenaline had us on the move, and we were anxious to get on with our escape. We had to force ourselves to temper the feeling of exuberance with the awareness that we were not yet free from danger. England and the United States were still far away, but we were over the biggest hurdle. I had the feeling we were winning a contest against unbelievable odds; the finish line was still in front of us, and we dared not let down.

After trying to climb the mountain to the swinging bridge, Clayton and "Scotty" David gave up and turned back. They settled for the postcard below which indicated the bridge is 173 meters (approximately 565 feet) above the floor of the stream bed. Clayton knew the climb had been difficult when he and the other three men with their Basque guide made it on that pitch black night in April 1944.

Chapter 15

Spain: Arrest and Internment

On the south side of the mountain where we were descending, the snow did not extend as far down as on the north side, where we had just come up. Water from the melting snow was trickling down the mountain, and we decided to follow it. We knew the trickling water would lead to a bigger stream and probably eventually to a road near the stream.

As we made our way down the mountain, we crossed the timberline and entered an area of trees and vegetation that helped to make our descent less obvious. Finally, light from the dawn replaced the moonlight. The dream of a new day in a new country became reality. From our briefings, we knew being in Spain could include some uncertainties and that though Spain was supposed to be a neutral country, our being there was risky; so we were mentally prepared for the situation.

As expected, the stream that had started out as a trickle from melting snow grew larger as we followed it down the mountain. Finally, we were low enough to see scattered houses, small farms, and country roads. At this point, we were not yet ready to become involved with the local residents, so we continued to follow the stream. It led us to a small village, where by now the people were up and the daily activities begun. The Spanish gendarmes were also up and active.

As we entered the outskirts of the village, two Spanish gendarmes were there to meet us. It was as if someone had spotted us earlier and alerted them to our coming. They were armed, and we knew immediately that our future was in their hands. They could not speak English any better than we could speak Spanish, so conversation was very limited. We did establish our identities as Americans and gave them our names. While they did not put us behind bars and were courteous to us, it was evident they had no intention of letting us proceed on our own.

In our presence, they made at least one phone call, and even though we did not understand the conversation, we could tell that they were checking with someone else to determine what they should do with us. I believe we were in the little village of Ochagavia. These gendarmes would be the ones to move us to a larger place. We did not see any police cars, and naturally we wondered how and when we would be moved. We did not wait long for our answers.

Two gendarmes soon had us waiting with them for a bus. When it arrived, it was not the kind of bus we had been accustomed to in the United States but an all-purpose vehicle loaded with produce as well as people. The inside of the bus was full, so we were obliged to sit on top among the crates of chickens, luggage, and other miscellaneous objects. While we held on to the railing around the top of the bus, the guards with their rifles did likewise. Together, we resembled a sheriff's posse riding shotgun with their prisoners in an old western movie. That was the way we traveled to another village where we got off, walked about one fourth of a mile, and waited in the shade of some trees for another bus.

On the next bus, we had seats inside, and the ride was more comfortable. We arrived in the city of Pamplona after dark. There we were escorted to a hostel, where the manager met us and took us to the second floor to join other American and British fliers for dinner. Our first day in Spain had just passed from the first stage, arrest, to the second stage, internment for an undetermined period of time.

At Pamplona, Sgt. Shaver and I were separated. He was taken to a large house with fenced surroundings at the edge of town and confined there with other non-commissioned officers. I remained with the other officers at the hostel in the middle of the city. We could go and come as we wished as long as we stayed inside the city limits. With adequate rooms and food, I began to have some sense of freedom. I enjoyed that feeling and the opportunity to be with others who had also been shot down and had escaped by various routes into Spain.

Early in the morning of my first day in Pamplona, the manager of the hostel had me in contact by phone with our American embassy in Madrid. They wanted my name, rank, serial number, and the approximate time and place at which I had entered Spain. They also wanted information on other Americans who had entered with me. This was referred to as "reporting in." It was the beginning of a formal process that would lead eventually to my being returned to England. A few hours after my phone contact, I received a call from the embassy. They reported that I had checked out OK with intelligence and that my parents would be informed that I was being interned in a neutral country. That was good news for me, and I knew my parents would be elated to hear something positive about my situation. For more than three months the only word they had received was the message, "Missing In Action."

After the embassy people had made my position clear, the conversation turned to S/Sgt. Kenneth D. Shaver. "How long did you know Sergeant Shaver before you entered Spain together? Where did you first meet him? Is there any question in your mind about his being an American?" After answering their questions and assuring them that he had to be an American, I asked, "What is the problem?" I was told he had been reported dead by the International Red Cross. I remembered then Ken's story of how he had had his dog tags in his flight jacket instead of around his neck while he was a prisoner of the Germans in Holland. When he and his fellow crew members had beaten up the guards and jumped off the train, he left his flight jacket behind. Apparently those dog tags were used to identify him as killed in the escape, not just as missing. After all, it is a serious charge against a military guard when prisoners escape.

The American embassy sent a man from their organization at Madrid to talk with Ken. The man was familiar with Ken's home town in North Carolina and interrogated him thoroughly in trying to confirm his identity. As a result of that visit, the embassy was confident that he was S/Sgt. Kenneth D. Shaver, and they treated him accordingly. However, it was not until after he returned to England and was identified by the intelligence officer of his base that Ken's wife was notified that he was alive.

While we were in Pamplona, an incident occurred which justified the need for caution in identifying men as Allied airmen. In this case, a man in the non-com camp was clearly a loner. He professed to be a French-speaking Canadian who knew no English. The American and English evaders found cause to doubt his story and created a situation to test him. Once, while he was standing near the perimeter of the grounds, one of the men moved in close to him without being noticed. When the American shouted, "Achtung!" (attention in German) the Canadian imposter snapped to attention. Realizing his true nationality had been established, he confessed to being a German soldier who had deserted, and he asked to remain with the group. He reported that he had been with the German Army on the eastern front fighting the Russians. Casualties were high on both sides, but it seemed to him that the losses the Germans inflicted, including men and tanks, were returned twofold by the Russians the following day. The futility of the situation and fear for his own life had caused him to desert. He had secured civilian clothes and escaped into Spain.

I believe he was permitted to remain with the Allies as a Canadian, but he was kept under guard and later flown blindfolded to England. There, intelligence could have a proper go at finding out as much as possible from him. His place as a prisoner of war in England would certainly be safer, and his life better than on the eastern front in Germany.

During my first few days in Pamplona I found out why we had not been moved on schedule from Paris. One of the American officers confided that the same organization that had helped Ken and me had got him through Paris just prior to our arrival at the school and church. He and others were safely escorted to Toulouse, France, and out into the mountains for their walk across into Spain. In spite of the checking which was done, a German had successfully infiltrated the group using American identification. By the time they reached the mountains, the infiltrator had learned all he could hope to about the organization, and so, as they rested one night, he slipped away and alerted German guards. They returned expecting to capture the entire group, and in the gun battle that followed many of the evaders and their helpers were killed, and some were taken prisoners. But my informant and one other man had been resting away from the group, and when the battle started, slipped away in the darkness and hid until it was all over and everyone had gone. Having been started in the right direction before the fight, the two succeeded in walking across the Pyrenees into Spain. Learning about that incident not only answered some questions for me, it made me more thankful than ever that we had gotten out of Paris and away from those who had helped us. At that point I could only hope the charges brought against Father Superior, the custodian, and the custodian's wife had not become more serious than the possesion of black market food, which was serious enough.

On my second day in Pamplona, I was interrogated by the Spanish military. They had a fort in Pamplona and trained soldiers there. The officer that attempted to interrogate me, however, was already a seasoned officer, a realist who knew his job and was courteous to me. The process began with a questionaire (in English) about my military organization, our equipment, where I was based, our target the day I was shot down, how we were shot down, and much more. I filled in my name, rank, and serial number as required and stopped.

When I refused to write in any other information, the Spanish officer tried to get me to answer the questions he put to me orally. He did speak English. He also tried a few tricky ways of getting information, but he was not abusive. The entire process continued for about an hour and a half. When it was clear I was going to tell him nothing but my name, rank, and serial number, he gave up in disgust and said, "Oh what the hell. It was all for the Germans anyway." I am sure he had been through this fruitless process with other officers of the Allied Forces. He was also sufficiently informed about the war to know the Germans were losing at this point, especially in the air.

Although Spain took on the status of a neutral country, it was easy to understand their sympathy with Germany. The Civil War in Spain had provided a testing ground for German arms and equipment and at the same time helped provide Franco with the winning margin which did not go unobserved by the officials of Franco's regime. It was not surprising that some of the Allied fliers who had tried escaping through Spain earlier in the war were imprisoned in undesirable conditions. Some of them were even turned over to the Germans.

There are indications that Spain even went through a bidding game between Germany and the Allies to see who would pay more for Allied evaders being held in Spain. In the latter part of the war the Allies offered petrol instead of money. That was an offer the Germans could not match, and was made at a time when the trend of the war favored the Allies as the eventual winners. Therefore, when I was in Spain, internment with a later release had become more routine — almost a sure thing. Time and the proper amount of petrol transferred to Spain would send me and others on our way to England.

Our embassy had also established a procedure permitting us to acquire some necessary clothing at a store in Pamplona. In addition, we received a few dollars each week for spending money. We could also draw some money against our pay if we desired. As we felt more freedom and adjusted to the situation, we could begin to enjoy some aspects of our internment and it offered some interesting incidents. One such enjoyable experience was shopping for new clothes.

The suit I had been given in Amsterdam was better than the clothing most of the men had been given, but I had worn it constantly for three months while traveling some tough terrain and in all kinds of weather. My G.I. shoes had been nearly new when I started, but the rocks and snow on the mountains had played havoc with them. I also needed a change of underwear, some socks, a couple of shirts, and a haircut to avoid looking like a drifter.

It was time to do something about my appearance. Another officer, who had been to the designated clothing store earlier, agreed to accompany me. I would select my clothes and have the embassy settle the account. That seemed simple enough until we discussed how I would communicate my needs to the clerk. It was agreed that I must try to use the few words of Spanish I knew, and he would help me if he could. After considerable effort on my part which included a lot of pointing, the lady clerk chuckled and began conversing in English. She had been through this experience before and enjoyed my struggle. She was an American. Her father was in management at the Sir Francis Drake Hotel in San Francisco. She and her mother had been visiting in Spain when the Spanish Civil War broke out and they had been detained there. She met, fell in love with, and married the man who owned and operated this store. They were delightful people and had several of us out to their place for dinner one day.

A store we visited on a more regular basis was the ice cream store. It was great to enjoy an ice cream cone and pastries after not having had them for many months. Getting an ice cream cone after siesta became a daily routine, and the young lady who waited on us seemed to look forward to our business. She tried hard to learn some English words, and we tried to learn Spanish. As it sometimes happens, she learned a few words of American slang that I fear may have had limited value to her.

Spanish soldiers would patronize the ice cream store once in a while, but the young lady was quick to point out how we were the more regular customers. The ice cream cones cost the equivalent of about five cents. That was almost identical to the amount the Spanish soldiers earned per day when they first entered service for training at the local fort. They were hesitant to blow a day's pay for an ice cream cone.

There had been a bullfight in Pamplona a few days before I arrived, and a number of the Allied fliers from the hostel had attended it. Their comments about the fight were interesting and varied, but I believe they found the running of the bulls to the arena the most unusual feature. At least that was the part of the event they talked about most. No bullfights occurred while I was there.

In Spain we would share a few of our past experiences when we felt certain our conversations would not be monitored. We learned about the variety of incidents that had brought us together in Spain. I met for example, a P-51 pilot who like so many fighter pilots had been escorting a formation of bombers when he was hit by German fighters. It was the first time he had bailed out in combat, but not his first time to hit the silk to save his life. He went down on the 5th of March in southern France and like the rest of us had escaped into Spain. Aviation, and particularly the United States, is fortunate that he survived to do a lot more flying. His name was Charles "Chuck" Yeager.

A British navigator with us in Spain was an interesting chap. The RAF made their bombing missions at night and did not fly in formation as we did. I believe most of the American fliers preferred to be in formation during the daylight hours, while the British fliers usually expressed satisfaction at going it alone under the cover of darkness without the big air battles which occurred during the day. The British fliers who bailed out at night were not as easily visible, but some of their night landings by parachute left much to be desired.

It was in Pamplona, while talking to an officer who went down after I did, that I learned Lt. Jack Watson had returned our burning plane to a base on the coast of England and survived without a scratch. The odds against that happening were unbelievable. My immediate thoughts were then, as they have remained, "Thank God he made it!" No good can come from wondering if we might all have gotten back had we stayed with the plane. There is no way to be sure, our best odds at the time favored the decision which was made.

After a couple of weeks in Pamplona, a group of us was moved to a large warm springs resort hotel at Alma de Aragon. We gave up some of the advantages of Pamplona for the pleasure of hot mineral baths and the exercise of rowing boats on a small lake. It was a smaller town than Pamplona with very narrow streets. There was a small theater in the village, and when they showed American films, the words were

*The **Stars and Stripes** in England announces the return of the burning plane.*

La Guardia Cables Hero Forgiveness For 'Buzzing' Game

1944

AN EIGHTH BOMBER STATION, Jan. 16—New York's Mayor, Fiorello La Guardia, has forgiven Lt. Jack Watson, of Indianapolis, for "buzzing" the Yankee Stadium while the World Series were in progress last Fall.

A wire came for the 21-year-old Fortress pilot soon after La Guardia heard of his performance last Tuesday when he brought back his B17, Meat Hound, on two engines, alone in the bomber, after instructing his crew to bail out. The wire read:

"Swell News. All forgiven for buzzing stadium. Congratulations and happy landings. Fiorello La Guardia."

The raid on Germany Tuesday was Watson's sixth. His No. 3 engine stopped just as the ship reached the target and soon after the No. 2 engine was set on fire by a direct hit from an FW190's 20mm. shell. The fire in the No. 2 engine nacelle later became so fierce that Watson was afraid the heat would reach the gas tanks and explode, so he told his crew to bail out.

Crewmen of returning bombers in the formation reported that six of the crew landed safely and the other three parachutes opened and were near the ground when they last saw them.

Alone in the bomber, Watson crash-landed his plane at an Eighth Fighter field near the English coast. Crews of GI firemen put out the fires before they reached the gas tanks.

The other three men in the "buzzing" incident are also in this theater. They are Lts. Jack Sheets, Tacoma, Wash.; Elmer Yong, Roachdale, Ind., and Joseph C. Wheeler, Fresno, Cal.

*The **Topeka Daily Capitol** reports, Lt. Clayton David lost over Holland.*

Lt. Clayton David Lost Over Holland

2/Lt. Clayton C. David, son of Mr. and Mrs. James C. David, route 6, was reported Saturday missing in aerial action over Holland since January 11.

Lieutenant David received his wings as a Flying Fortress pilot at the Altus, Ok., Army airfield last summer. He has two brothers in service, Floyd J. David, in the Navy, and John E. David, Army.

written in Spanish across the bottom of the screen.

If I had any illusions about Spanish senoritas being overly warm and sexy, some reality came to light at this location. The ladies who worked at this hotel were friendly and interested in exchanging comments about their culture and ours. Their dating offered quite a contrast to ours according to what we were told. When their young ladies went out on a date, mama went along until the time the couple publicly announced their engagement. While we were there, one of the young ladies working at the hotel became engaged to her boy friend of many months. One of the ladies with whom she worked came in kidding her about matrimony. Naturally we were interested in how soon the wedding would take place. Our inquiry was a simple, "Pronto?" (soon).

Her reply was, "Mucho pronto!" (very soon).

Our next question was with regard to the number of days, "Cuantos dias?"

To that she answered, "No dias, dos-tres anos." (two or three years).

Then we began to understand something about their thoughts on the length of a courtship and probably the accumulation of a dowry. I found myself hoping my stay in Spain would not last for as many months as a short courtship in Spain, and it didn't.

I had been there about a month, which was long enough to receive one letter from home, when I learned I would be on my way to England. Several of us were picked up in a couple of cars from the embassy in Madrid and driven to the embassy. It was an interesting trip, and we drove through the plains where much of the Civil War fighting had occurred, and where the damage from the fighting was clearly visible.

Our trip to Madrid took place on a Sunday, so there was limited activity at the embassy when we arrived late in the afternoon. We were exposed to some questions which I remember as being more of a curious than an interrogative nature. It was great to be back in American hands! However, this was not the place to celebrate or be too obvious to the eyes of the natives. That evening, we were escorted to the train and given good accommodations for an overnight ride that would get us to Gibraltar the following day.

Money was kept as a souvenir of countries visited. The Metro ticket above is from a Paris subway. The four small tickets (center, right) are U.S.A. ration coupons.

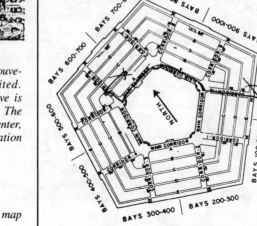

Right, 1944 visitor's map for the Pentagon.

The two pictures at the right were taken in Spain. Those in the picture at lower right are Charles B. Screws, James E. Williams, Dale W. Kinert, Harry C. Yarwood, Bernard W. Rawlings, William Guyn (Dutch), Roy W. Carpenter, Jr., Howard J. Mays, and Clayton David on right first row.

Paper money, above and opposite, was often signed by friends and was then called "Short Snorter."

Chapter 16

Return to England

While we were on the train headed toward Gibraltar, dawn revealed orchards of olives and oranges, a warm and peaceful sight, which I enjoyed very much. From the train I also saw for the first time a forest of cork trees and could observe how the cork was harvested. The entire setting was far removed from the war, and it had me wishing there was time to get off the train and stroll in the beauty of the countryside.

The train could not go all the way to the Rock, and our last few miles were by car. As we entered that British facility, it was quite evident Gibraltar was basically a military establishment. After we checked in and received our billeting, British intelligence officers took us through some debriefing exercises that could help them spot the unusual and might supply new information to update what they already knew about escape lines and the enemy.

Our three days on the Rock provided some interesting sights and some transition back to military living. We were issued some make-do uniforms, and we turned in the civilian clothing we had secured in Pamplona. We understood the civilian clothing would be boxed up and returned to Pamplona or to a similar place in hopes other evaders could or would use it — the idea being to avoid buying all new clothes for everyone. It impressed me as an optimistic and economical gesture, but I wondered what really happened to the clothing during the chain of events.

While on the Rock, we learned something about British customs. We watched the guards each evening as they went through their traditional ceremony of closing and locking the gate which led to the mainland of Spain.

Our stay at Gibraltar gave me my first chance to stand on one continent and be able to look across a body of water at another continent. As I stood one day on a peak of the Rock and looked across the Strait of Gibraltar to Spanish Morocco, the value of having the

British in control of the Rock took on added meaning for me. In one sense, the Rock is one big fortress, honeycombed to make it as functional as possible for military purposes, with powerful guns that could be aimed at potential targets in almost any direction.

The value of Gibraltar as a port and trade center was also visible. I enjoyed the bananas, oranges, and other fresh fruits available in the markets and on the streets. As strategic as the location was for military purposes, the commerce, the view, and the weather almost made me envy the people who were assigned there.

My stay on the Rock was a short one. The evening of the third day, I was taken down to the airport for a plane ride back to England. The airport was, as it remains, one runway along the side of the rock that faces Spain. Takeoffs and landings are limited to the two opposite directions. When the strip is in use, the road across it that carries traffic between Spain and Gibraltar must be closed. In some ways it resembles an aircraft carrier. You are going to get very wet or worse if the plane is not airborne when you reach the end of the runway on takeoff. Overshooting the runway on landing is just as disastrous.

Our transportation was the old faithful C-47 with passenger seats. The flight was made over water and some distance from the coastline to make it safer. In order to increase its range and flying time, the plane was not heavily loaded. On board with several of us who had been interned was a guard with a blindfolded prisoner. Our vision was also limited, as curtains were drawn on all the cabin windows to make certain that not even the smallest amount of light would be emitted accidently, making us visible in the night sky and endangering our flight. We certainly didn't want to be picked off by a German night fighter at that point, not after we had survived so much and were so close to being back in England.

At day break we landed safely in England some distance southwest of London. From the airport we took a train to London and checked in at an assigned hotel within walking distance of Piccadilly Circus.

On the train to London I sat across from two English ladies. Each one had a son that appeared to be about eight years old. When their conversation turned to comments about the war, I heard them talk about shortages and the hardships the war had created. One of the ladies pointed to her son and said, "He can't remember what a banana or a fresh orange tastes like." Less than 18 hours before, I had been where they were plentiful. How I wished I might have been able to reach into my duffel bag and pull out bananas or oranges for those young lads. But our mission was secret, and we were encouraged to take or say nothing that might reveal where we had been.

Positive identification was the first thing which occurred in London before we could be permitted out of the sight of military personnel. Jack Watson arrived from our base to identify me, and it was a great relief to see him. I was pleased to see him wearing captain's bars but shocked to see that his beautiful black hair had turned mostly grey during the four and one half months we had been separated. It was now the 25th of May and I had bailed out on the 11th of January. Naturally, we had more to talk about than we could cover during our first time together again. We would have a lot to talk about later.

Another pleasant surprise greeted me in London. It was a footlocker containing all my clothes and belongings. When I had not returned from the mission, the officers of the crew with which I trained had assisted in gathering up my belongings. The articles had then been put in a footlocker and sent to a depot for storage. When it was learned that I would be arriving in London, the footlocker was delivered to the hotel. I was more fortunate than most, since I had been housed with the officers from my training crew, and they were there to look out for my interests. It took a crew reunion 40 years later before I could thank them in person. They had been shot down three days after me. They all survived their jump but ended up as prisoners of war.

My debriefing in London was very thoroughly and professionally done. The female officer who did it had traveled on the continent before the war and had actually visited the school where we had been in Paris. She apparently had a record of the inquiries my helpers had made with intelligence in England. She was so thorough in her interrogation that I had the feeling she knew more than I did about where I had been. My confidence in the intelligence branch of service was enhanced by that experience.

From our debriefing at the hotel in London, we were sent out to S.H.A.F. (Strategic Headquarters for Allied Forces) for physical examinations. The medics found me in excellent health. I felt great, but not all of the returning airmen were so fortunate. Some of them suffered from wounds that had not been treated properly and others were experiencing the ill effects of confinement or improper nutrition.

That the men who had experienced any exposure to the German gun placements along the French coast or missile launch sites were promptly interviewed by intelligence at S.H.A.F. gave me the impression we were getting close to the time of the invasion. When the streets of London contained only a few military men because most were restricted to base with their units, I was certain the time for the invasion was near.

Staying in London a few extra days for my records to be cleared and to receive my promotion orders also gave me a chance to see more of London. The British navigator who had been with us in Spain returned to England on the same flight I did from Gibraltar. He went immediately to his base but agreed to come back to London one night and take a couple of us on a visit to Scotland Yard. He had been working there when he entered the war. True to his word, he came in the third night we were in London and told us he had been back over Berlin the night before. The British were short of fliers, and they wasted no time in returning their evadees to combat. The inspectors at Scotland Yard were pleased to see their friend had made it back from "Missing In Action." They provided the three of us a most enjoyable and interesting evening at their pub.

On the 6th of June, several of us left our hotel in London for breakfast at a nearby USO club. As we were walking, we heard a flight of bombers overhead, and we looked up. They were flying formation in a configuration different than normal. This had to mean the invasion had begun. Anxious to learn as much as we could as quickly as possible, we ate our breakfast and caught the subway out to S.H.A.F. where we could expect accurate information. Our timing was excellent. As we entered headquarters, General Eisenhower's famous announcement of the invasion was being given over the public address system. Our speculation about the invasion was confirmed. I wanted to return to my base near Molesworth and learn what was happening, so I caught a train out of London.

Chapter 17

The Faith of
Family and Friends

At my base, I had an opportunity to catch up on the news about friends and learn about activities. First I learned we had lost 109 men the day I bailed out. Up until then I was the only one who had succeeded in evading and returning to the base. During our air battle, it had appeared doubtful that there could be any survivors from several of the planes that blew up that day, though there had been a report of one or more survivors off every crew except one. The reports were coming through the International Red Cross regarding men who had become prisoners of war. Our 303rd Bomb Group had been awarded a Presidential Citation for extraordinary heroism, determination, and esprit de corps in action against the enemy for that day, 11 January 1944.

Most of the men I knew were no longer around the base. A few had completed their missions and returned to the states, but 11 January and the missions that followed had taken their toll. The strain showed in the faces of the men who had been flying missions more frequently in preparation for, and now in support of, the invasion. I asked if I should volunteer to go back on operations. I felt better, and I was more rested than most of the men. The answer was, "No!" At least two risks were involved if we should be shot down again and captured. With a crew of ten men we could all experience severe treatment in an effort to learn about my escape. Also, in the best interest of those who had helped me, I could not risk the possibility of giving out information under torture. My records, like those of most evaders, were marked for no further duty in a war zone outside the continental United States.

While at the base, Jack Watson and I made one local flight. Flying out over the Channel for a look at the invasion was not possible: returning pilots reported the weather was preventing them from seeing the ocean or the front lines. I did view some of the photos that had been taken from planes in the group, and they were impressive. The photo lab and intelligence were kind enough to let me have pictures of our plane which had appeared in the paper, *Stars and Stripes*. The pictures showed how the plane had been damaged and was foamed down to put out the fire after Watson had landed it at the coast. It was a bit unnerving to learn they had recovered an unexploded 20mm shell from under the pilot's seat. Our lives would have been very uncertain if that shell had exploded, so I am grateful that German manufacturing was not perfect!

When I visited the Squadron Mail Room to see if I had any mail, I was in for a great surprise. From the day I went down until they learned I was in a neutral country and would be returning, my mail had been stamped "Missing In Action," and returned to sender. A number of letters for me had arrived during the last month. As the mail clerk handed them to me he remarked about the faith of some people and how he would stamp letters to be returned to the sender only to have them followed by a new supply. In my case, this had gone on for months. When I returned home, this was confirmed by a stack of letters which my mother had written to me — one every week — and which had been returned.

When I was at the Air Base near Topeka, Kansas, before going to England in early November 1943, my brother Floyd, a Navy pilot, was home on his way to a new assignment in the states. We discussed the risks which we both knew existed in combat flying. I had expressed my confidence in being able to make my 25 missions or escape if shot down. I asked for his support in keeping the spirits up at home if I was ever reported "Missing In Action." I expected to walk out and return. We already had another brother, John, who was crew chief on the ground with the Air Force in India. He had been out of the United States since November 1941 and it had required a lot of faith to endure the long periods when the family did not hear from him.

Our mother had the kind of faith that gave her the strength to take it in stride when our youngest brother, Maynard, signed up to become a bombardier on B-29's. He was later sent to Tinian, in the Marianas Islands, and flew missions to Japan. Mother's faith was so great she helped Dad keep his chin up during the worst of days with four sons in the service. All of us had duty in war zones outside the United States. We all came home safely and saw our parents proudly displaying the emblem in the window with four stars on it.

After my visit to the base at Molesworth, I returned to London to receive both my travel and promotion orders. Then I got a flight from London to Prestwick, Scotland, where I remained overnight. London had been quiet while I was there, but the first buzz bombs hit London the night I was at Prestwick. I was glad to be on my way to the United States and a visit with my parents at home.

Where I had been and how I had escaped was classified as "Secret" information. That made for some interesting incidents with friends who knew I had been missing. Some would stare as though they might be seeing a ghost. Others would start asking all kinds of questions. I would just make some comment about bailing out of a burning plane and getting back. Then I would change the subject.

When I called a friend in St. Louis with whom I had previously worked, he wanted to know where I was calling from. We chuckled over that question several times as the years passed. It had been as if he was expecting me to answer either "Heaven" or "Hell," and he wasn't sure which.

I had always understood that it was possible to escape from or evade the enemy's grasp, but the odds were never talked about. I have since learned that of the fliers reported as "Missing In Action" over western Europe, about one half became prisoners of war. About one half of the MIA's were later reported "Killed In Action." Only about one out of every 100 of us fliers reported as MIA's escaped or evaded capture and returned. We have just cause to be thankful for what we were able to achieve and to appreciate the faith of those who prayed and waited.

Chapter 18

Return to Duty

When I returned to the United States, the plane landed at Washington, D.C., and my orders were to report to intelligence at the Pentagon. I was taken to their nearby location in Virginia, where I was to present my story to a group of officers, some of them experienced personnel, some in an intelligence training program. As I walked in, they were hearing final comments from Kenneth Shaver. He immediately acknowledged me as the man who had traveled with him from near Maastricht into Spain. After hearing my story, they asked us both to return to their unit after we had had our days of leave at home. We would assist them in briefing combat air crews going to the European theater of operations. Ken and I both agreed to their request and immediately left for our respective homes, Ken to see his wife in North Carolina and I to see my folks in Kansas.

It was more than a month later when Ken and I met back in Washington, D.C., for our temporary assignment with intelligence. As we faced the hot muggy weather of summer without air conditioning, we had plenty of time to review our past experiences and talk about what had happened on our return home. Ken told what it was like to go home to a wife who had lived for months thinking he had been killed. That is what she had been told after Ken's escape from the Germans in November. She was not told differently until after his positive identification in England, so she had only waited about two weeks for his return.

While at home Ken read the communications his wife, Birdie, had received when he was missing in action and the one saying he was dead. I believe his biggest shock was a visit to the cemetery where he saw a stone erected in his memory at an empty grave. We hope that grave remains empty for many years to come.

I have always found physical activity a help to me in making adjustments, so it was fortunate I returned home when there was alfalfa hay to be cut and put in the barn. With so many men in the service, labor was scarce, and neighbors worked together to harvest crops. I was able to pitch right in and be a renewed part of my family and the neighborhood for a few days before reporting back to duty.

Talking about an unusual situation can also help one adjust, but we could not use that approach with most of our friends because our experiences were classified "Secret." Therefore, I am thankful for the opportunity Ken and I had to share our experiences with some of the aircrews before they left for England and Europe. It was done in cooperation with intelligence and had their approval. I believe it helped me adjust to what we had been through, and it gave the crews insight into one of the potential aspects of combat.

When my temporary assignment with the intelligence unit was complete, it was back to the cockpit for me. First I trained to instruct other pilots to fly the B-17. Then I transferred to the Ferry Command, where I checked out in several other types of planes, including fighters. When the war ended in Europe, and later when it ended in the Pacific, I was flying new airplanes which were the best United States had built up to that time. I flew them from the factories where they were made to various locations in the states where they were pickled for storage. Some of them would never fly again and be scrapped, while many of the P-51's in particular would survive and be sent to Korea years later.

Finally, after the war with Japan was over, the day came when my total duty points meant I had a decision to make. I chose to be separated from active service and restart my life as a civilian where my bride, "Scotty," and I could be together. We had been married 11 February 1945. I accepted my reserve commission and continued to make myself available for recall for more than 20 years. I retired from the reserves as a lieutenant colonel.

My long walk to freedom those few trying months was laced with danger for me and those who risked their lives to help me. It was an important part of my life and an experience I hope I never have to repeat for any amount of money. However, if my freedom is threatened I will find a way to do something about it because I am convinced that if the day comes when we are unwilling to fight for our freedom, that will be the day when we begin to lose our freedom!

A Tribute to My Helpers

Helping the Allied airmen was a high-risk contribution to the resistance effort, and many fine people of Europe paid with their lives when they were caught. Some were promptly executed, while others were tried beforehand. Many died in concentration camps or survived the camps to die soon thereafter as a result of their mistreatment. It is well known that the Germans applied their own severe rules in the concentration camps while generally following the rules of the Geneva Conference in their handling of the Prisoners of War. The difference takes nothing away from the hardships suffered by the thousands of Allied airmen who became POW's. But it does account for the difference in the survival rates.

I know more than 60 people helped me in one way or another while I was evading. This was an unusually large number of helpers due to the great distance I traveled behind the enemy lines and the fact that we were almost captured in Paris.

As is the case with most other Evaders, I have never been able to identify accurately or locate some of my helpers. Odds are that some of those who remain unknown did not survive. There were those I know did not survive, and some of the survivors died after the war without my having much information about them.

The ways in which people helped, took risks, and expended effort varied greatly among helpers. Some provided food, others information, clothes, money for train tickets, a hiding spot, housing, or a finger pointed in the right direction. Some children and adults helped by keeping their mouths shut about our presence. Then there are those who were our personal guides. They often helped in all the ways others helped us and in addition risked being seen with us in public.

Every single bit of help I received was important to me then and now. It was the combination of all the pieces that made it possible for me to survive and evade. In recognition of all my helpers, and as a tribute to those who helped downed Allied airmen all over Europe, it has been a pleasure for me to be able to research and write this book. It has been stimulating for me to include comments about and from some of my helpers, their experiences and their achievements. While it would require a thick book to do some of these individuals justice, I hope the vignettes included in this book have helped you, the reader, better understand the people who risked their lives to resist German occupation and aid the Allies. Most of my helpers resisted the Germans by helping people like myself in a humanitarian way. They kept trying to make something good for mankind come out of the war.

The amount of information available to me about each of these individuals varies greatly. Therefore, the amount I have written also varies, but individually and collectively these are true heroes and heroines to many people and especially to me. The honors given and the stories written about them will never tell it all, but history is made and recorded through the lives of those who live it. Living with these people through life-threatening experiences and being able to join some of them in sharing the joys of freedom has given me a broader understanding of how freedom evolves and the price often paid for it.

Freedom, like other things of great value, takes on the greatest meaning to those who experience losing it. You understand the meaning of freedom if you have walked beside those willing to risk everything, including life itself, to regain it. My successful walk to freedom remains a tribute to those who walked beside me and made it possible. We did it together!